Stra...
Q

MARCUS GARVEY

By
Omowale Pert-em-Hru

 **Ukombozii**
Education for Liberation
Afrikan Freedom Means Defeating Neo-Colonialism
www.ukombozii.org

Omowale Ru Pert-em-Hru

Pan-Afrikanism: From Programme to Philosophy

Original Booklet Cover

Omowale Ru Pert-em-Hru

Pan-Afrikanism: From Programme to Philosophy

Strategically Selected Quotes From

Marcus Garvey

Omowale Ru Pert-em-Hru

Copyright © 2020
Omowale Ru Pert-em-Hru

All rights reserved.

ISBN- 13: 979-8600829442

Published by
Omowale Ru Pert-em-Hru

Ukombozii@gmail.com
00 44 (0) 7933 145 393

Pan-Afrikanism: From Programme to Philosophy

Pan-Afrikan Society Community Forum (PASCF) Ancestors:
Forerunner organisation to Ukombozii:

Brother Omowale

• *Brother Ras Lloyd* (aka Lloyd Johnson) the first *Chair of the PASCF* – Born 17th August 1956, crossed to meet the ancestors 20th December 2011;

• *Brother Oxalando Efuntola* (aka Andrew Navarro Smith) the first *Director of Communications* and *Organisational Priest* of the PASCF – Born 29th January 1957, crossed to meet the ancestors 16th September 2014; and

• *Sister Mawasi Bojang* (aka Patricia Presilla Chambers) the first *Deputy Chair of the PASCF*, who took up the role of *Chair of the PASCF* on the passing of Ras Lloyd – Born 8th February 1965, crossed to meet the ancestors 11th May 2016.

Though our comrades did not necessarily describe themselves as socialists, they were all ardent, committed and active anti-imperialists. They all gave selflessly to the struggle against capitalism and made important dedicated contributions to our people's advance towards socialism within the disciplined framework of organised resistance.

In part, this document comes out of their practical grounded work experience. We thank them for their contributions to the liberation of our people – each of them a solid rock in our struggle. They will always be remembered by the PASCF and Ukombozii.

Omowale Ru Pert-em-Hru

Table of Contents

Preamble 3
  My Vision for Afrika and her people 3
    Our capacity to create, produce and build as our contribution to a better world for humanity 3
    Driven by our capacity to govern a just society for Afrikan people .. 4
    Driven by our capacity to build respectful relationships for the achievement of happiness 5
    Driven by a humble and respectful relationship with our environment for the achievement of higher understanding 6

1 Introduction 13
  1.1 The booklet's purpose 13
  1.2 Structure of the quotes 13
  1.3 A note on alterations 15

2 Understanding the essence of Marcus Garvey 17
  2.1 What Garvey stood for 17
  2.2 Garvey's organisation: The UNIA 18
  2.3 The role of Afrikan women in the UNIA 19
  2.4 Garvey's Pan-Afrikanist nation building agenda 20
  2.5 Garvey opposed Elitism & Exploitation in all their forms 20

3 Afrikan people 23
  3.1 Identity for unity and liberation 23
  3.2 Identity is deeper than nationality or citizenship 24
  3.3 History – a foundation for Identity 25

4 Some Revolutionary Afrikan personality traits 27
  4.1 Integrity of character 27
  4.2 Women in the struggle 28

5 The People's problem 31
  5.1 Genocide – Colonisation as a means to extermination 31
  5.2 Assisting in our own oppression 34

5.3 A problem solving response 35

6 Solution: strategic aim and objective 37
6.1 The people's universal strategic aim 37
6.2 Afrikan people's strategic national objective 38

7 Organising Afrikan people for liberation 41
7.1 Organisation for protection, survival and self-determination 41
7.1.1 Disorganisation invites destruction 41
7.1.2 Arming through organisation 42
7.1.3 Other nations are not ours 43
7.1.4 Organising for an Afrikan nation 44
7.1.5 Solid unity from effective organisation 46
7.2 Educating Afrikan people for enhanced organisation 48
7.2.1 Learning to change the world 48
7.2.2 Education for enhanced organisation 49
7.3 Religion and Afrikan liberation 50
7.3.1 Garvey's personal beliefs 50
7.3.2 Managing religion for unity 51
7.3.3 Religion as the oppressor's tool 51
7.4 In defence of the organisation 52
7.4.1 Enemy within (the organisation) 52
7.4.2 Enemy within (the race) 54
7.4.3 Enemy without 55
7.4.4 Counter attack 56

8 Organisational relations with outsiders 59
8.1 Afrikan people are our primary concern 59
8.2 Building alliances 60
8.3 Acts of solidarity 60
8.4 Attitude towards non-Afrikans 61
8.5 On Lenin 62
8.6 Separatism as a tactic 64
8.7 Excluding non-Afrikans from meetings 64

9 Reparations and Repatriation 67
   9.1 Reparations..67
   9.2 Repatriation 69

10 Measures of Achievement..73
   10.1 Organisational..73
   10.2 Personal 74

11 Contextual issues 77
   11.1 The central Importance of Afrika 77
   11.2 The critically important impact of World War I 80
   11.3 Revolution..82
   11.4 Hints of armed Struggle 83

Omowale Ru Pert-em-Hru

ACKNOWLEDGMENTS

To the Charles, Peltier, Emmanuel, Daniel, Lewis, Michel, Pascale, Bougyne, Ramey lines and all of our unknown ancestors right back to our origin in Afrika. Without all of you and each of you individually, our present day lineage could not exist; nor could anything that we've produced, including this book. Though I can never repay my debt to you, I can contribute to the recovery of Afrika by passing your gift of life to the next generation in a manner that will make us proud. Thank you for life and much, much more.

It is now 8pm on Wednesday 15th November 2017, the 19th anniversary of the passing of Kwame Ture. I worked with but never met him. He is one of my ideological fathers. The redrafting of this book will be completed tomorrow, the 47th anniversary of the passing of my father John Baptist Charles a.k.a. Agee, Kenagee or Senford. My debt to both fathers mentioned here is eternal.

.

Preamble

My Vision for Afrika and her people

Our capacity to create, produce and build as our contribution to a better world for humanity
I want every Afrikan person on earth to be an effective contributor to the technological advance of humanity and the production of ever more effective and efficient tools. What we are going to achieve with our mastery of new technology is beyond anything that we can currently imagine, but some of the indicators of our advance will include:
- The reproduction of ever healthier people symbolised by 100% live women and babies emerging from the birthing process and Afrikan babies born with an average life expectancy in excess of 100 years;
- The production of ever more intelligent/productive people symbolised by:
    - The understanding that Afrika – the richest land in the world – will remain under the exclusive sovereign control of Afrikan people at home and abroad collectively into eternity;
    - Afrikan children's complete mastery of the history/geography of Afrika and the world;

- Afrikan children's complete mastery of the secrets of quantum physics;
  - Afrikan children's complete mastery of the ability to bring the past and future into the present and work on them to create an optimally better future;
  - Afrikan children's complete mastery of the languages and techniques of efficient and effective communication;
  - Afrikan children's complete mastery of managing our continent and the world for the greater good of humanity and Mother Nature;
- The production of ever higher and better technology i.e. tools in service of and in harmony with the best interests of humanity and Mother Nature, symbolised by an ever cleaner planet, in turn symbolised by the ability to produce and reproduce an abundance of:
  - The purest and freshest possible air;
  - The purest and cleanest possible water;
  - The healthiest and most nutritious foods;
  - The most robust travel vehicles facilitating the movement of Afrikan people through the universe at speeds faster than the speed of light;
  - The most efficient and effective long and short distance communication tools;
- By living in a world where:
  - We fully deploy the creative genius of Afrikan people to produce all that we need (and surplus) so effectively, efficiently and speedily that we create more time for us to respectfully engage with each other, Mother Nature and our ancestors; and
  - The most advanced technologies flourish in service of Afrikan people as part of greater humanity and Mother Nature.

Driven by our capacity to govern a just society for Afrikan people
I want every Afrikan person on earth to understand that the most effective method for governing our homeland and people at this point in history means:

- Afrika, including her surrounding islands, must be united and governed as one continental-wide super-state, freed from all internal 'national' boarders;
- The super-state must be created by and be under the collective control of all Afrikan people – those at home and those abroad – and predominantly managed by women;
- The land and resources of Afrika must be under the exclusive sovereign control of Afrikan people at home and abroad collectively and used for the benefit of all Afrikan people in the first instance, making us the richest, most powerful people and humble leaders of the world for the greater good of humanity;
- We must develop a military capability sufficient to defend our homeland from any foe;
- Our continental-wide super-nation-state - the most powerful in the world - is constantly ready, willing and able to protect any and all of her children whether based at home or abroad;
- Our continental-wide super-nation-state is a means to a greater end. It is tasked with laying the foundation for a continent and by extension a world so supportive and in tune with the best interests of the people, Mother Nature and our ancestors, where truth, freedom, justice and peace are so inculcated into human existence, that all states become unnecessary, are removed from the world and become relics of history.

Driven by our capacity to build respectful relationships for the achievement of happiness

I want every Afrikan person on earth to understand, adopt and apply in the modern world the principles underpinning the tendency towards healthy relationships found typically in Afrikan village culture. Namely that:
- Human beings are fundamentally humble and respectful of other human beings, Mother Nature and their ancestors;
- Every human being is more important than property, money or profit and therefore an end in their own right, not a means to somebody else's end;
- The benefits to the 'we' are usually, but not always, prioritised over the benefits to the 'me' and when the benefits to the 'me' are given higher priority, that is decided by the 'we'; and

- Whilst all human beings are unique have differing qualities, attributes and abilities, we are all equal in essence;

Driven by a humble and respectful relationship with our environment for the achievement of higher understanding

I want every Afrikan person on earth to understand that:
- Mother Nature is composed of antagonistic opposites held in unison;
- The never ending engagement of opposites is the source of perpetual change in Mother Nature and everything in her;
- Mother Nature was there before us and gave us space within her;
- We are a part of Mother Nature;
- We are absolutely obliged to engage with Mother Nature;
- Spirit is inside Mother Nature;
- Spirituality is the process of connecting with spirit, achievable only through a respectful engagement with Mother Nature;

Agreement/acceptance with/of the above vision will form part of the criteria for membership of Ukomozii. It is to be recited twice daily (first thing in the morning and last thing at night) by all members and their families as a constant ongoing reminder of the future that unites us.

Omowale Ru Pert-em-Hru
19th January 2018

Pan-Afrikanism: From Programme to Philosophy

Omowale Ru Pert-em-Hru

"But I think that of all the literature that I studied, the book that did more for me than any other to fire my enthusiasm was the *Philosophy and Opinions of Marcus Garvey* published in 1923." **Kwame Nkrumah (End)**

"He [Marcus Garvey] was the first man, on a mass scale and level, to give millions of [Afrikans] a sense of dignity and destiny, and make the [Afrikan] feel that he was somebody." **Martin Luther King (End)**

"And if it were not for the tendentious ideas of Marcus Garvey – the blazing star around which thousands of satellites revolve, who appears to have the talent of attracting the [Afrikan] population of [US Satan]; if it were not for his ideas, in my view condemnable only for unjustified ambition – I repeat, who better than he would defend the rights of the [Afrikan], whether in haughty England or in any other place where his powerful voice might resound." **Juvenal A Lopez de C Cabral – father of Amilcar Cabral (End)**

"Every time you see another nation on the Afrikan continent become independent, you know that Marcus Garvey is alive." **Malcolm X (End)**

Pan-Afrikanism: From Programme to Philosophy

Omowale Ru Pert-em-Hru

Strategically selected quotes from Marcus Garvey

1 Introduction

1.1 The booklet's purpose
This booklet *Strategically Selected Quotes from Marcus Garvey* is intended as a handbook for members of the **Pan-Afrikan Society Community Forum (PASCF), Sankofa360°Ltd, Ukombozii and similar organisations** to assist them in the speedy assimilation of Garvey's key strategic ideas. Beyond that it is hoped that it will also contribute, by performing a similar role in the wider Afrikan community and among friends and supporters of the Afrikan liberation struggle.

1.2 Structure of the quotes
Thanks to the effective organisation of our recent ancestors, the history of Marcus Garvey and the UNIA is well documented. That said, it appears that very little work has been done on decoding their strategic approach. Garvey was constantly involved in political skirmishes. One

of the consequences of this is that they have become so prominent, so well documented and attracted so much attention that the corresponding distraction partially obscuring his far sighted strategic approach – an approach which remains relevant to the present day. The quotes have therefore been selected, arranged and structured in a manner attempting to give some indication of the UNIA's underlying Afrikan Liberation Strategy.

The outline structure for the quotes is as follows: firstly, the constituency is defined; secondly, a few positive personality traits are noted along with the role of women; thirdly, the main problem confronting Afrikan people - the constituency - is demonstrated; fourthly, quotes identifying the UNIA's universal aim and strategic objective are presented; fifthly, quotes expressing the importance of effective organisation are presented. Many different facets contribute to the effective operation of organisations and with that in mind quotes on unity, education, religious practices and enemy behaviour are considered under this important banner. Organisational relations with outsiders are also considered; as is the UNIA's repatriation agenda, together with quotes suggesting some kind of measure of achievement.

Important contextual issues that impact upon strategy are also highlighted including the centrality and importance of Afrika and its massive wealth on the people's problems and potential solution; the overarching influence of World War I; Revolution and armed liberation struggle. Garvey's words hinting at 'armed struggle' or more precisely fighting to the death for Afrikan people's freedom, are not generally well known. When Amy Jacques Garvey published *The Philosophy and Opinions of Marcus Garvey: Or, Africa for the Africans* in 1925, Marcus was an unjustly incarcerated political prisoner – having been the victim of a US Satan kangaroo court. The primary objective at that point was to get him out. It is therefore understandable that his words on subjects such as 'brute force,' 'bloodshed' and 'liberty or death' were tactically excluded from that compilation. Some of those words are included in this booklet.

Finally, quotes illustrative of Garvey and the UNIA's claim for reparations made on behalf of Afrikan people are included. These examples are instructive in that they were made before the term 'reparations' even existed, yet they remain relevant to contemporary campaigns on the issue. The incorporated quotes are drawn mainly, but not exclusively, from the highpoint of the UNIA's activism i.e. 1919 to 1922; a few are drawn from the lessons of Garvey's Afrikan School of Philosophy. A brief outline of the UNIA's strategic approach to Afrikan liberation is presented below as a backdrop to the structure guiding the presentation of the quotes in this booklet.

1.3 A note on alterations
The quotes in this document are direct quotes from Marcus Garvey. They are extracted from his public speeches or documents that he signed. Some adjustments have been deliberately made. For instance, the 'N' word which was the currency of the time has been replaced with '[Afrikan];' the more vulgar version has been replaced with '[N].' In some, but not all cases, the words 'coloured' and 'black' have been replaced with '[Afrikan].' Where Garvey has stated his organisation's name in long hand, the initials or term 'UNIA' has been inserted. It is accepted that these alterations introduce a level of distortion. Language, which in any event is not neutral, changes over time and the object, for better or worse, is to give the quotes a more contemporary meaning – one that is less offensive to Afrikan people currently struggling with the issue of their identity.

The term '[US Satan]' has been inserted for 'United States of America.' This is to give emphasis to its character as the vilest nation-state in the history of humanity. In order to come into being, it exterminated the Native Americans in a genocidal frenzy, followed immediately by another horrendous act of genocide – this time against Afrikan people. It is the only nation-state to be born of a double genocide and is apparently proud of it. From its settler colonial origin it has continued in its unrelenting, unrepentant anti-human imperialistic downward path, with little to no suggestion of an unforced change on the horizon. In essence, it started off in the worse possible way and from there, it simply degenerated.

Omowale Ru Pert-em-Hru

Strategically selected quotes from Marcus Garvey

2 Understanding the essence of Marcus Garvey

2.1 What Garvey stood for

Marcus Garvey stood for the unification and liberation of Afrika and her people under a just social system. He understood that Afrikan people were one people regardless of whether they were born at home in Afrika or overseas in the Afrikan Diaspora. The essential point was that Afrikan people had to unite and organise on the basis of their Afrikaness to achieve the common purpose of Afrikan liberation. For Garvey the liberation of Afrika meant that Afrikan people at home in Afrika would live their lives in an environment of self-government with unfettered liberty, political freedom and democracy. Afrikan people who chose to live in foreign lands would have the protection of their Afrikan government at home.

Garvey was building an inter-continental or Pan-Afrikanist organisation, centred in Afrika that would be willing to fight to the death to achieve Afrikan self-determination. In order to achieve this Pan-Afrikanist aim, Garvey had to sweep aside all opposition, whether internal i.e. from within the Afrikan community or external from the forces of imperialism that dominated Afrika and the rest of the world. This position put him into direct opposition with the European invaders that illegitimately occupied, colonised and controlled the Afrikan continent and other parts of the world. He was therefore, locked into a life and death battle with the imperialist controllers of the world. It was this that gave momentum to the anti-colonial dimension of Garvey and the UNIA. This is the reason why the anti-colonial and anti-imperial elements of Garvey's approach are essential to a correct understanding of his ideas.

2.2 Garvey's organisation: The UNIA

The engine of the Garvey movement was effective inter-continental or Pan-Afrikanist mass organisation amongst Afrikan people. Garvey was more than a mere advocate of effective Pan-Afrikanist organisation, his whole life stood as a testimony to it. He was, without a doubt, among the most accomplished organisers, of his era, both in the Afrikan liberation movement and beyond. He packed halls and arenas during his speaking tours; but more importantly he had the ability to translate packed halls into effective organisational activity aimed at advancing Afrikan people. He scientifically employed political, historical and cultural education programmes to encourage Afrikan people to join his organisation and to develop their consciousness once they were members. In this way their labour became a more effective tool in the Afrikan liberation process. In 1923 he assessed the membership of this organisation at 6 million, a figure which he later estimated rose to the height of 11 million.

His formidable organisation the Universal Negro Improvement Association & African Communities League (UNIA) established branches on 5 continents and developed its own independent: headquarters – Liberty Hall in New York; mass conventions – with up to 25,000 Afrikan people in attendance; defence force – including the beginnings of an air force; nursing organisation; youth section or juvenile division – which was to produce a future president of the UNIA; fleet of ships; weekly newspaper - which was the most widely distributed Afrikan newspaper in the world; 'Declaration of rights'; Afrikan Orthodox Church; School of

Afrikan Philosophy and business corporation comprising factories and a chain of retail outlets. With the assistance of allies, the UNIA even managed to gain a voice at the League of Nations – forerunner to the United Nations.

2.3 The role of Afrikan women in the UNIA

A critical feature of the UNIA was the fact that it challenged the entrenched sexist order of the day with more than 50% of its membership being Afrikan women. The UNIA stipulated that a substantial proportion of the senior positions in the organisation were occupied by Afrikan women; every chapter had to have 'Lady President' and 'Lady Vice-President' positions. Afrikan women such as: Amy Ashwood Garvey, Amy Jacques Garvey, Henrietta Vinton Davis, Lora Kofey, Lillian Galloway, Madame De Mena, Queen Mother Moore and Mittie Maud Lena Gordon to name a few all occupied positions of considerable power in the UNIA including the positions of leader and joint leader.

Strategy of Garveyism

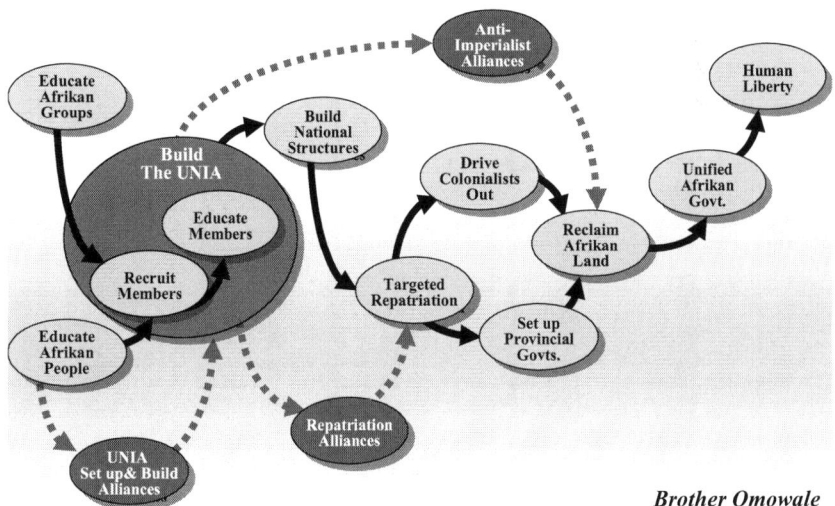

Brother Omowale

The UNIA also had sections which were the special preserve of Afrikan women. The Universal Afrikan Motor Corps was part of the UNIA defence corps. It was the only women's paramilitary organisation known to be operating in North America. Similarly, the Black Cross Nurses formed part of the health infrastructure of the UNIA, with a role to play in times of peace and war. Whilst these accomplishments did not mean that the organisation was free from sexism, it is evidence that the power of Afrikan women was relatively well utilised in the pursuit of Afrikan liberation. It also affirms that in many respects Afrikan women were the backbone of the organisation.

2.4 Garvey's Pan-Afrikanist nation building agenda
It is important to note that Garvey was not building the organisation for organisation's sake. Garvey had an aim. Through the utilisation of scientific methodologies, he was seeking to build a thriving continental wide sovereign Afrikan nation-state with a civilisation of its own. Within that context, Garvey was building national structures through the various projects being developed via the UNIA; he was laying the foundations for a unified Pan-Afrikanist national government together with the essential ingredients of its defence force and its economy. These Pan-Afrikanist structures would be transplanted back into Afrika as part of the centrally co-ordinated mass repatriation programme for those Diasporan Afrikan people who decided that they could best serve their people by returning home to Afrika. However, Garvey warned returning Afrikan people that the reason for their return was to contribute to the rebuilding of the Afrikan nation and not to exercise an elitist lordship over their sisters and brothers already resident in the Afrikan motherland.

2.5 Garvey opposed Elitism & Exploitation in all their forms
Anywhere that Afrikan people faced the elitist superiority of racism and colonialism, Garvey opposed it. Anywhere that Garvey found the elitist superiority of self-appointed Afrikan leadership in the Afrikan community, Garvey opposed it. In fact anywhere any people were ravaged by the unjust elitist system of colonialism, Garvey opposed it. Garvey opposed elitist ideas and practices both within and between races. He was openly opposed to elitism based on race, class or any combination of the two. Garvey continually emphasised the fact that whilst he stood resolutely for justice for Afrikan people as the most oppressed group of people in the world, he was not opposed to other races of peoples. He pledged that the UNIA would fight for the 'great goal' and 'common cause' of humanity – that of justice for all oppressed peoples. Through his famous slogan 'Afrika for the Afrikans' he made Afrika primary amongst his considerations; he stood by the agenda of

'race first' and not 'Afrikan race only'. It was this approach that provided the basis for Garvey's anti-imperialist alliances with non-Afrikan groupings.

Omowale Ru Pert-em-Hru

Strategically selected quotes from Marcus Garvey

3 Afrikan people

3.1 Identity for unity and liberation

"We of the UNIA are determined to unite 400,000,000 [Afrikans] for their own industrial, political, social and religious emancipation ... we are determined to unite the 400,000,000 [Afrikans] of the world for the purpose of building a civilization of their own. And in that effort we desire to bring together the 15,000,000 of the [US Satan], the 180,000,000 in Asia, the West Indies and Central and South America, and the 200,000,000 in Afrika. We are looking toward political freedom on the continent of Afrika, the land of our fathers." (Garvey, 1986, p. 95)

"The programme of the UNIA is the drawing together, into one universal whole, all the [Afrikan] peoples of the world, with prejudice towards none. We desire to have every shade of our colour, even those with one drop of Afrikan blood, in our fold; because we believe that none of us, as we are, is responsible for our birth; in a word, we have no prejudice against ourselves in race. We believe that every [Afrikan person] racially is just alike, and, therefore we have no distinction to make, hence wherever you see the UNIA you will find us giving every member of our race an equal chance and opportunity to make good." **(End)**

"... the UNIA embraces [Afrikan people] everywhere; that the UNIA has no national bar, no colour bar, where [Afrikan people] are concerned. The UNIA is not insular; not parochial, is not national, is not Barbadian, is not Jamaican, is not Trinidadian, is not American; it is purely an [Afrikan] institution. When you join the UNIA, you will not join it as a Barbadian, Jamaican, Trinidadian, American, you join it as an [Afrikan]. And we recognise anyone as [an Afrikan] who has one 16th drop of [Afrikan] blood in his veins. If he does not claim to be [an Afrikan] he may stay to himself and we welcome him to stay there; hence you realise, I am here representing not an insular institution, not a parochial institution, not a national institution, but a universal movement for [Afrikan people], that is Universal Afrika for [Afrikan people], by [Afrikan people], a government of our own. Barbadians can work for it, Jamaicans can work for it, Americans can work for it; just as you worked for the Panama canal." **(End)**

3.2 Identity is deeper than nationality or citizenship

"God almighty gave you a country – the richest and most prolific among all the continents. He gave you the great continent of Afrika. It is for you to repossess yourselves of it. Remember, men, the Afrikan is in each and every one of us coloured men. We cannot get away from it if we tried. One sixteenth of the bloo[d] makes you an Afrikan and we cannot get away from it. Therefore do not play the fool and talk about your not being an Afrikan. All of us are Afrikans. But the only difference is: some are Afrikans at home and others are Afrikans abroad. We are the Afrikans abroad, unfortunately. Why, I am so sorry I was born abroad! I wish I was born at home; there could be some trouble here today. I was born in an alien country ..." **(End)**

"All [Afrikans], whether in [US Satan], the West Indies, South and

Central America or Afrika, have but one common parentage ..." **(End)**

"Everybody knows that there is absolutely no difference between the native Afrikan and the American and West Indian [Afrikans], in that we are descendants from one common family stock. It is only a matter of accident that we have been divided and kept apart for over three hundred years, but it is felt that when the time has come for us to get back together, we shall do so in the spirit of brotherly love, and any [Afrikan] who expects that he will be assisted here, there or anywhere by the UNIA to exercise a haughty superiority over the fellows of his own race, makes a tremendous mistake. Such men had better remain where they are and not attempt to become in any way interested in the higher development of Afrika." **(End)**

"Now, let us go back to the natur[al] existence of the individual. I had a Black mother and a Black father. Can you imagine that you could have conceived me as a British first before I was conceived as an offspring? Just argue that out for yourselves. How impossible it is for a man to be first a nationality before he was completely born. He was part of a man and part of God's own image before he was brought to see the light of day, therefore he must first be of his race before he could be of his nation." **(End)**

"I am not an Englishman by race, I am a Britisher by nationality. Just as you are true to your Anglo-Saxon race and type – and you would be unworthy if you were not – so am I true to my Afrikan race and Afrikan type ... Before a man is born to a nation he is conceived to a race; so his nationality is only accident whilst his race is positive ... God intended us to have different outlooks from the social and political points of view; that is why geographically he suited you for Europe and me for Afrika.." **(End)**

"... you have made me by compulsion a British subject, when by election I would be an Afrikan citizen ...." **(End)**

3.3 History – a foundation for Identity

"A people without knowledge of their past history, origin and culture is like a tree without roots". **(End).**

"Every falsehood told by the historian should be unearthed ..." **(End)**

"The history of the movement is now being written. Do you know what history means? History is the guidepost of a race; is the inspiration for succeeding generations either to go forward or to stand still either to revenge or be revenged." **(End)**

Strategically selected quotes from Marcus Garvey

4 Some Revolutionary Afrikan personality traits

4.1 Integrity of character

"It is not my purpose to deceive the world. I believe in righteousness; I believe in truth; I believe in honesty." **(End)**

"I trust no one from my people would believe that I could be so mean as to defraud my fellow [Afrikan person], either directly or indirectly. I have an ideal that is far above money, and it is to see my people really free.

Others of my race oppose me because they fear my influence among the people, and they judge me from their own corrupt, selfish consciences." **(End)**

"The greatest prop to character is honesty. Honesty is the best policy. Let no one believe that you are dishonest. If they believe that you are dishonest, you are doomed. You will never be able to rise to a position of respect and trust except by some mere accident. You must live so clean that everybody can see the cleanliness of your life.

Never let people believe that you are a liar, but the contrary. Let them believe that you always speak the truth and live up to it." **(End)**

"… a leader must be honest. You have your character to maintain. You can maintain it only by good conduct. Therefore, never try to fool anybody or deceive any body.

Never fabricate or falsify; if the thought should ever come to you, count the consequence and the risk. It may be your last chance, and it may be your first mistake. Most men suffer from their first mistake; from which they never recover." **(End)**

"… If you have won your cause by a lie, then as early as possible, try to make the cause right, but only after you have won; for no cause can continue successfully without righteousness …" **(End)**.

"If these things were said under my signature I am responsible." **(End)**

4.2 Women in the struggle

"We say that the time for Afrikan women to leave the kitchen is now." **(End)**

"Among those who I can recommend as being the most honourable and consistent leaders of the movement are two women who have done exceedingly well, when nearly all men have failed, and they are still in active s[e]rvice – Madame MLT DeMena, who is our present international organ[iz]er, and Lady Henrietta Vinton Davis, who is our present secretary general. We have had very little trouble with the women in the movement; with the exception of one or two, we have never had a dishonest woman in the leadership of the organisation. Every Wom[a]n has played fair and true. But it is sad to say that nearly every man we placed in [a] position of trust ha[s] abused the confidence and proven a scamp. They always see the selfish 'I,' the desire to exploit the people willing to support the cause, and for their own purpose." **(End)**

Omowale Ru Pert-em-Hru

Strategically selected quotes from Marcus Garvey

5 The People's problem

5.1 Genocide – Colonisation as a means to extermination

"For over three hundred years the white man has been our oppressor, and he naturally is not going to liberate us to the higher freedom – the truer liberty – the truer Democracy. We have to liberate ourselves." **(End)**

"The attitude of the white race is to subjugate, to exploit, and if necessary exterminate the weaker peoples with whom they come into contact.

They subjugate first, if the weaker peoples will stand for it; then they exploit, and if they will not stand for SUBJUGATION nor EXPLOITATION, the other recourse is EXTERMINATION." **(End)**

"There is a world-wide effort for the subjugation, the exploitation and ultimate extermination of the weaker peoples of the world. This plot has been laid for some time. It is now being engineered in all seriousness by several of the well developed and powerful races of today. It means that in another short while – not so short in the sense of time as we count it, but in the sense which historians reckon it – in a short while, in another few hundred years it is calculated that only a certain race will occupy this world. That is to me the fittest race; the only race that believes itself worthy of surviving; the race that you know as I do, that is proud, haughty, arrogant; that race that hates to see anyone else but those of its own kind advance and rise in the scale of civilisation. There is a serious plot laid, and that is engineered that only that class of people, that type of people, that race of people, will be found here in another couple or few hundred years, except the weaker peoples, the underdeveloped peoples get together now, in their own habitats and among themselves, to see that their rights are protected and their liberty insured forever. The average mind cannot understand, the average mind cannot grasp the significance and the importance of the situation; not even the ordinary mind of that group that is engineering this plot knows anything about it, because all changes that are beneficial to the group, to the race or to the nation, are generally engineered by those who have been selected by the group or the race or the nation to do the thinking ... as the [US Satan] white man has multiplied in [US Satan] within the last few hundred years from a few hundred to nearly 100,000,000, so will the other races in the world multiply from 1,500,000,000 to probably 5 billion in another 500 or 1,000 years. As an increase of 90,000,000 could not occupy the same space as 90,000,000 in [US Satan] now occupy, so when in years to come the human race has multiplied considerably new room must be found for those who have multiplied in this larger number. It means, therefore, that the race that is strong or that has become more numerous, as that race becomes more numerous and weaker races exist alongside of them they will ultimately push off the weaker races to make room for the growing stronger races of which they are members. It means that [US Satan] does not grow larger to accommodate the increasing number which the 90,000,000 will multiply to, so the world will not become larger to accommodate all of the one race, and in another 500 or 1,000 years it will mean a question of survival of the fittest race.

That is the end towards which all races of the world is tending, and the race that fails to read the signs of the times, to prepare itself, will only open itself to great dangers and perils in the future. That is why people in India, under the leadership of Ghandi, are determined to have India free. That is why the Nationalist Party of Ireland is determined to have complete Irish independence.

I am warning you in Liberty Hall and throughout the world, except you and I and all of us together now make Afrika the national home of the [Afrikan], in another two hundred years we will find absolutely no accommodation on this globe of ours. That is the situation. As the white man of Europe came here hundreds of years ago and settled down and ultimately exterminated the North American Indian, so it is that he has set out and gone into Afrika to settle down. There are 6,000 whites in East Afrika to a population of 4,000,000 natives, and except these natives get together, in another 200 years you will have 4,000,000 whites and 6,000 natives. That is what it means and that is why a fight must be made now and must be made, not by others, but must be made by you. And that is why the UNIA appeals to the loyalty of its members everywhere. We may think that we are not concerned because we live in [US Satan] and because we live in the West Indian islands. Let me tell you, men, that in [US Satan], in another hundred years will be no place for the [Afrikan]. It is the intention of the white man to get rid of us, and except we get together to protect our interest, not only in [US Satan], but throughout the world, by building up a mighty nation in Afrika which will stand the test of time, your position and mine and the position of your children will never be permanently secured in the world.

That is the whole situation of the race. You need not look for hope, and that is why I am so stubborn and determined that the [Afrikan] must have a nation of his own. That is why I am so determined that Afrika shall be redeemed and that we shall have a government there second to none, so that when the strong races seek to exterminate us, when they make up their minds to wage a battle for the survival of the fittest, you and I will stand here until Gabriel blows his horn.

It is no use trusting to chance. Six thousand men are now holding down four million! Why? Because they have only sticks and stone[s], while the other six thousand people have bayonets and other things. The idea is to get possession of everything that the other man has now. That is the thought I want to get into the minds of the [Afrikan] peoples of the world. Therefore, this is not the time for you to remain around here fighting and bickering with each other. This is the time for us to present to the world the best within us – the best technically, scientifically and in every way, because we are drawing near to the period of the survival of the fittest." **(End)**

"I feel sure that those of you who will pay keen attention and study to political events will realise that a dangerous scheme is being engineered in Europe to defeat the plans of [Afrikans] in redeeming Afrika. Afrika is to become a common battleground of the exploiters – the exploiters who are now looking towards Afrika as the only redeemer, as the only saviour, and they realise that a change is coming about among those who claim ownership of Afrika. The change is that those who claim ownership of Afrika are crying out 'Afrika for the Afrikans,' and those people who desire Afrika have entered into a conspiracy to further darken or becloud the eyes of [Afrikans] and turn their attention from independence in Afrika. They talk about mandatories in Afrika; it means nothing else but another hundred years of merciless exploitation of the natives and the wealth of Afrika; and they are now about to use certain coloured men – certain [Afrikans] to defeat the intention of the far-seeing members of this race of ours." **(End)**

5.2 Assisting in our own oppression

"All people are struggling to blast a way through industrial monopoly of races and nations, but the [Afrikan] as a whole has failed to grasp its true significance and seems to delight in filling only that place created for him by the white man." **(End)**

"The traitor of other races is generally confined to the mediocre or irresponsible individual, but, unfortunately, the traitors among the [Afrikan] race are generally to be found among the men highest placed in education and society, the fellows who can call themselves leaders.

For us to examine ourselves thoroughly as a people we will find that we have more traitors than leaders, because nearly everyone who essays to lead the race at this time does so by first establishing himself as the pet of some philanthropist of another race, to whom he will go and debase his race in the worse form, humiliate his own manhood, and thereby win the sympathy of the 'great benefactor', who will dictate to him what he should do in the leadership of the [Afrikan] race." **(End)**

5.3 A problem solving response

"I read 'Up From Slavery,' by Booker T. Washington, and then my doom -- if I may so call it -- of being a race leader dawned upon me in London after I had travelled through almost half of Europe.

I asked, 'Where is the black man's Government?' 'Where is his King and his kingdom?' 'Where is his President, his country, and his ambassador, his army, his navy, his men of big affairs?' I could not find them, and then I declared, 'I will help to make them.'

Becoming naturally restless for the opportunity of doing something [for] the advancement of my race, I was determined that the black man would not continue to be kicked about by all the other races and nations of the world, as I saw it in the West Indies, South and Central America and Europe, and as I read of it in America." **(End)**

Omowale Ru Pert-em-Hru

Strategically selected quotes from Marcus Garvey

6 Solution: strategic aim and objective

6.1 The people's universal strategic aim

"We who make up the UNIA have decided that we shall go forward, upward and onward toward the great goal of human liberty. We have determined among ourselves that all barriers placed in the way of our progress must be removed, must be cleared away for we desire to see the light of a brighter day ... Men of other races and nations have become alarmed at this attitude of the [Afrikan] in his desire to do things for himself and by himself." **(End)**

"The UNIA stands for the Bigger Brotherhood; the UNIA stands for human rights, not only for [Afrikans], but for all races. The UNIA believes in the rights of not only the black race, but the white race, the yellow race and the brown race. The UNIA believes that the white man has as much right to be considered, the yellow man has as much right to be considered, the brown man has as much right to be considered as well as the black man of Afrika. In view of the fact that the black man of Afrika has contributed as much to the world as the white man of Europe, and the brown man and yellow man of Asia, we of the UNIA demand that the white, yellow and brown races give to the black man his place in the civilization of the world. We ask for nothing more than the rights of 400,000,000 [Afrikans]." **(End)**

"We represent peace, harmony, love, human sympathy, human rights and human justice, and that is why we fight so much. Wheresoever human rights are denied to any group, wheresoever justice is denied to any group, there the UNIA finds a cause. And at this time among all the peoples of the world, the group that suffers most from injustice, the group that is denied most of those rights that belong to all humanity, is the black group of 400,000,000. Because of that injustice, because of that denial of our rights, we go forth under the leadership of the One who is always on the side of right to fight the common cause of humanity ... so under the leadership of the UNIA, we are marshaling the 400,000,000 [Afrikans] of the world to fight for the emancipation of the race and of the redemption of the country of our fathers." **(End)**

"All intelligent people know that one's nationality has nothing to do with great ideals and principles ... great principles, great ideals know no nationality." **(End)**

6.2 Afrikan people's strategic national objective

"... the UNIA has been advocating the cause of Afrika for the Afrikans - that is, that the [Afrikan] peoples of the world should concentrate upon the object of building up for themselves a great nation in Afrika." **(End)**

"We declare to the world that Afrika must be free, that the entire [Afrikan] race must be emancipated from industrial bondage, peonage and serfdom; we make no compromise, we make no apology in this our declaration." **(End)**

"... surely we have not forgotten to fight for ourselves, and when the time comes that the world will again give Afrika an opportunity for freedom, surely 400,000,000 black men will march out on the battle plains of Afrika, under the colors of the red, the black and the green ...

We shall march out in answer to the cry of our fathers, who cry out to us for the redemption of our own country, our motherland, Afrika." **(End)**

"... we are coming four hundred million strong, and we mean to take every square inch of the twelve million square miles of Afrikan territory ... we are out to get what has belonged to us politically, socially, economically and in every way." **(End)**

"We are organized for the absolute purpose of bettering our condition, industrially, commercially, socially, religiously and politically. We are organized not to hate other men, but to lift ourselves, and to demand respect of all humanity." **(End)**

"We are not engaged in politics because we have enough local politicians, Democrats, Socialists, Soviets, etc., and the political situation is well taken care of. We are not engaged in domestic politics, in church building or in social uplift work, but we are engaged in nation building." **(End)**

Strategically selected quotes from Marcus Garvey

7 Organising Afrikan people for liberation

7.1 Organisation for protection, survival and self-determination
7.1.1 Disorganisation invites destruction

"Organise now or perish" **(End)**

"The greatest weapon used against [Afrikan people] is disorganisation." **(End)**.

"... the mighty forces of the world are operating against non-organised groups of peoples, who are not ambitious enough to protect their own interests." **(End)**.

"The political readjustment of the world means that those people who are not sufficiently able, not sufficiently prepared, will be at the mercy of the organised classes ..." **(End)**.

"... we are preaching the doctrine of preparedness to the [Afrikans] throughout the world. Prepare with financial power; prepare with physical power; prepare with educational power; prepare with scientific power. The only way you can combat the organised powers of the world now lined up for the exploitation of Afrika and of this race of ours is to keep yourselves in a position where you can meet fire with hell fire." **(End)**

"The cause of this organisation shall come first to me in all my deliberations." **(End)**.

"The [Afrikan person] cannot protect himself living alone – he must organise. When you offend one white man in [US Satan], you offend 90 million white men. When you offend one [Afrikan person], the other [Afrikan people] are unconcerned because we are not organised. Not until you can offer protection to your race, as the white man offers protection to his race will you be a free and independent people in this world." **(End)**

7.1.2 Arming through organisation

"... your strongest armament is organisation ..." **(End)**.

"[Afrikan people] must arm through organisation." **(End)**.

"You do not need to have guns and bombs just now; you have no immediate use for them ..." **(End)**.

"I am not asking you to arm with the things that they have, I am asking you to arm through organisation; arm through preparedness ... Their weapon in the past has been big guns and explosive shells; your weapon must be universal organisation. You are a people most favourably situated today for getting what you want through organisation." **(End)**.

"... brute force is the thing that rules the world; not religion, not politics, but brute force, and if you have an organisation you will get brute force as quickly as you can ... Brute force – the power to knock somebody out of the way. It is the power that England has, and if you want to retire her you will have to get superior power, and that is what the UNIA is organised for – to get 400,000,000 [Afrikans] together. And one month after that is done 30,000,000 Anglo-Saxons will hold themselves in that little island called England and never show themselves around the 12,000,000 square miles of land called Afrika. So long as you keep disorganised, so long as they keep up this bluff, and I trust that the Third International Convention of the [Afrikans] of the world is going to give us an organisation that will be perfect for its physical strength, so that when we call upon the entire race we will act as one man." **(End)**

"... you were once great; you shall be great again. Lose not courage, lose not faith, go forward. The thing to do is to get organised and you will compel the world to respect you. If the world fails to give you consideration, because you are [Afrikan people] ... you shall through organisation shake the pillars of the universe and bring down creation ..." **(End)**.

7.1.3 Other nations are not ours

"We want only those things that belong to the [Afrikan] race. Afrika is ours. To win Afrika we will give up America, we will give up our claim in all other parts of the world; but we must have Afrika. We will give up the vain desire of having a seat in the White House in America, of having a seat in the House of Lords in England, of being president of France for the chance and opportunity of filling these positions in a country of our own." **(End)**

"If the [Afrikan] were to live in this western hemisphere for another five hundred years he would still be outnumbered by the other races who are prejudiced against him. He cannot resort to the government for protection for government will be in the hands of the majority of the people who are prejudiced against him, hence for the [Afrikan] to depend on the ballot and his industrial progress alone, will be hopeless as it will not help him when he is lynched, burned, jim-crowed and segregated." **(End)**

"Do they lynch Englishmen, Frenchmen, Germans or Japanese? No. And why? Because these people are represented by great governments, mighty nations and empires, strongly organised. Yes, and ever ready to shed the last drop of blood and spend the last penny in the national treasury to protect the honour and integrity of a citizen outraged anywhere ... Until the [Afrikan] reaches this point of national independence, all he does as a race will count for naught ..." **(End)**.

"Nationhood is the only means by which modern civilisation can completely protect itself ... Independence of nationality, independence of government, is the means of protecting not only the individual, but the group ... Nationhood is the highest ideal of all races. **(End)**.

"... every careful student of political science can foresee a future of tears for those that are not prepared to defend themselves by strong organisation. When we say political organisation, we do not mean as confined to one's domestic district, where you live, as the subject or citizen of the Government that is controlled by an alien race. We mean political organisation that is indeed independent to race, that political organisation that will make you an independent political unit among the nations and races of the world. We mean the political organisation called independent government." **(End)**

"You may argue that [the Afrikan] can use his industrial wealth and his ballot to force his government to recognise him, but he must understand that the government is the people. That the majority of the people dictate the policy of governments, and if the majority are against a measure, a thing or a race, then the government is impotent to protect that measure, thing or race." **(End)**.

7.1.4 Organising for an Afrikan nation

"Show me a well organised nation, and I will show you a people and a nation respected by the world." **(End)**.

"For five years the UNIA has been advocating the cause of Afrika for the Afrikans, that is, that [Afrikan] peoples of the world should concentrate upon the object of building up for themselves a great nation in Afrika ..." **(End))**.

"The difference between the UNIA and other movements of this country is that the UNIA seeks independent government while the other organisations seek to make the [Afrikan] a secondary part of existing governments." **(End)**.

"Races and people are only safeguarded when they are strong enough to protect themselves, and that is why we appeal to the four hundred million [Afrikans] of the world to come together for self-protection and self-preservation." **(End)**

"Organisation is the force that rules the world. All peoples have gained their freedom through organised force. All nations all empires have grown into greatness through organised methods. These are the means by which we as a race, will climb to greatness. The world around us is organising itself today. The white world of Europe is so organised as to be able to protect itself from foreign invasion. Asia is organising to repel the aggressor. Afrika at home and abroad are the only open doors that suggest exploitation and robbery to othe[r] peoples. When I say Afrika at home, I mean the 280,000,000 of Blacks who live on the continent that God gave us as our heritage. There we have no well organised government for protection. Because of that all alien races of Europe have invaded that territory and they have subjugated the teeming millions to serfdom, to slavery. Afrika abroad is suffering from many abuses. In [US Satan] we have the lynch rope around our necks. In the West Indian islands we are relegated to the ditch of industrial stagnation. Nowhere in this br[o]ad universe are we recognised as a competent race simply because we have failed in the most essential weapon – organisation. Let us be organised in Brooklyn tonight as we are organised in other parts of the country and in the West Indies. ["] This war that has been won by the allied nations was fought for a great principle. It was that of giving all peoples the right to govern themselves. Now that there is peace and the affairs of the world are to be settled, we find that every race except the [Afrikan] will have a voice in the principle of self-determination. And why is it so? Because all of them are organised [.] In the matter of comparison, you can hardly find any race of people standing on the same political platform as the [Afrikan]. They might suffer disadvantages, such as Poland, but none of these countries suffer in the way that Afrika suffers. Afrika of 12,000,000 square miles is the most congenial country in the world for [Afrikan people] … every spot that is habitable has [become?] the domain of the white man, and he has possessed himself of it, not by matter of conquest alone, but through the easiest methods possible, simply because there has been no organised resistance. The time for the peaceful penetration of the Black man by the white man is past and the time for a determined resistance has come, and it is on that platform that we of the UNIA stand. We are determined to live and die free men. Men who are free never admit of inroads into their rights. When such inroads are attempted, the result has always been a fight to the finish. When Germany made her inroad into the political boundaries of Northern Europe, there was an organised resistance to repel her. She has been whipped, and I am now saying to you people in Brooklyn tonight that the same methods that were used by the allied governments in whipping Germany to her knees for the intrusion that she had made into the rights of other people's, is the same course that we must take as a universal people to repel the aggressor on the continent of Afrika. Afrika will be a bloody battlefield in years to come. We cannot tell who the foemen will be, whether he be English, French, German, Belgian or Dutch; but there is one thing we are determined on that we are going to fight it out with him to a finish. That finish must mean victory for the Afrikan standard.

Freedom has become a sacred possession for men. No race can be completely free, living as subjects of an alien race. The [Afrikan] is tired of being a subject. He is tired of being a citizen without rights, and the time is now ripe when we should guarantee freedom even at the cost of our lives. One generation must die in half even to save the other generation in whole. As for me the spirit of Patrick Henry still moves; it is the spirit of liberty or death. There has always been one consolation for me which I gained out of this war. I, as a young man, could have died in France, in Flanders or Mesopotamia, fighting for the brutal Belgian. Since I could have died without achieving anything for myself after the victory, I am now resolved to try the game of dying for myself; but before I die, I feel sure that my blood will have paid that remission for which future generations of the [Afrikan] race shall be declared free. Freedom of action, freedom of opportunity are things we need, which I believe can only be gained after we shall have established an imperial power to command respect of nations and races." **(End)**

7.1.5 Solid unity from effective organisation

"... because [Afrikan people] are suffering all over the world we feel that the time has come for four hundred millions of us scattered all over the world to link up our sentiment for one common purpose – to obtain liberty and democracy." **(End)**

"If we must have justice, we must be strong; if we must be strong, we must come together, we can only do so through the system of organisation ... When we successfully bring together the 400,000,000 [Afrikans] of the world, we will have not only racial, collective and individual justice, but national justice as well." **(End)**.

"We are endeavouring to unite [Afrikan People] everywhere, and for what? For the purpose of building up a powerful nation on the continent of Afrika, a nation in the near future boasting as a first-rate power, and that first-rate power to give us Afrikan citizens, who domicile ourselves in [US Satan] as Afro-Americans, the protection which America does not give us today. That is the larger purpose of the UNIA ... We have left nothing out of this UNIA because we realise that other nations have left nothing out where their progress is concerned. We are endeavouring to perform the function of government for our race, just as the Government of [US Satan] performs the functions of government for ninety million white people." **(End)**

"We 400 million Black people desire, late though it may be, to restore ourselves to the company of nations, with honour, so that we may show the way to the real peace that these commercial statesmen are talking today, but do not mean, except to the extent of more oil monopolies, more diamond monopolies, more rubber concessions, more disarming of the weaker peoples whose lands are so valuable as to supply them, the monopolist, with the resources and wealth that they need." **(End)**

"I want you to understand that you have an association that is one of the greatest movements in the world. The New [Afrikan], backed up by the UNIA, is determined to restore Afrika to the world, and you scattered children of Afrika in Newport News, you children of Ethiopia, I want you to understand that the call is now made to you ... we in the UNIA intend within the next 12 months to roll up a sentiment in [US Satan] that will be backed by 15 million Black folks, so that when in future you touch one [Afrikan] in Newport News you shall have touched fifteen million people, so that when you touch any [Afrikan] in Newport News you touch four hundred million [Afrikans] all over the world at the same time." **(End)**

"Today the spectacle of millions of [Afrikans] from Afrika, America, the West Indies and other parts of the world, stretching forth their hands to each other in token of blood-brotherhood, with grim determination to break down the bars that impede their progress, haunts the dreams of their oppressors and strikes terror to their hearts. It is a fact of common knowledge that where there is unity there is strength, and if I mistake not the tone and temper of the white nations of the world, they undoubtedly recognise the power of organisation. Let no man deceive you; 400,000,000 {Afrikans} when united constitute a power that must be reckoned with. That this fact has been recognised is evidenced in the strenuous efforts put forth to prevent the consummation of unity among the [Afrikans] of the world. That these efforts have failed and are forever doomed to failure is evidenced in the Greatest Convention of [Afrikans] now holding its sessions in Liberty Hall and numbering among its delegates men and women from all parts of the world who are discussing the various problems confronting us, with a view to taking remedial action for their soluti[on]. That [Afrikans] have learned the value of organisation and the necessity for racial unity and integrity is further evidenced in the splendid response now most strikingly manifested in the unparalleled achievements of the UNIA and its associate bodies." **(End)**

"Let no religious scruples, no political machinations divide us, but let us hold together under all climes and in every country ..." **(End)**

7.2 Educating Afrikan people for enhanced organisation
7.2.1 Learning to change the world

"Education is the medium by which people are prepared for the creation of their own civilisation, and the advance and glory of their own race." **(End)**

"All good psychologists realise that if you can set a man thinking that you are likely to produce, through him, results that never would have been possible otherwise. The object I have in view is to get the [Afrikan] to accomplish much for himself out of his own thoughtfulness. To arouse that thoughtfulness, he must be shocked or otherwise he must be driven to see the unusual that is operating against him ..." **(End)**

"If we had not a complete training in knowledge before 1914 in that we only knew the book and were only able to read and write, they of themselves gave us training and placed two million of us in the army and gave us gun and gun powder and taught us how to use them. That completed the education of the [Afrikan]. Therefore, tonight the [Afrikan] stands complete in Education. He knows how to read his book, he knows how to figure out, and he knows how to use the sword and gun. And because he can do these things so splendidly, he is determined that he shall carve the way for himself to true liberty and democracy which the white man denied him after he was called out to shed his blood on the battlefields of France and Flanders." **(End)**

7.2.2 Education for enhanced organisation

"Read! read! read! and never stop until you discover the knowledge of the Universe." **(End)**

"Read history incessantly until you master it. This means your own national history, the history of the world, social history, industrial history, and the history of different sciences; but primarily, the history of man. If you do not know what went on before you came here and what is happening at the time you live, but away from you, you will not know the world and will be ignorant of the world and mankind.

You can only make the best out of life by knowing and understanding it. To know, you must fall back on the intelligence of others who came before you and left their records behind." **(End)**

"In reading it is not necessary or compulsory that you agree with everything you read. You must always use or apply your own reasoning to what you have read based on what you already know as touching the facts on what you have read. Pass judgement on what you read based upon these facts. When I say facts I mean things that cannot be disputed. You may read thoughts that are old, and opinions that are old and have changed since they were written. You must always search to find out the latest facts on that particular subject and only when these facts are consistently maintained in what you read should you agree with them, otherwise you are entitled to your opinion ... Read through at least one book every week, separate and distinct from your newspapers and journals. It will mean that at the end of the year you will have read fifty-two different subjects. After five years you will have read over two hundred and fifty books ... never forget that intelligence rules the world and ignorance carries the burden. Therefore remove yourself as far away from ignorance as possible and seek as much as possible to be intelligent." **(End)**

7.3 Religion and Afrikan liberation
7.3.1 Garvey's personal beliefs

"We declare for the freedom of religious worship." **(End)**

"The white man tells us in his lying scriptures – and I want you to understand me clearly on this, I am as much a Christian as any Pope of Rome, I am as much a Christian as the Arch Bishop of Canterbury, I am as much as Jesus Christ, but I refuse to believe all of the lying stuff that the white man put in the bible." **(End)**

"Religiously, we are still slaves to the doctrine of an alien race. It is true that a large number of us here tonight from [US Satan], the West Indies, Canada, South and Central America are Christians, whilst others of us are Mohammedans, but for us Christians, have we ever stopped to question the source of our religion; that whilst there is nothing wrong with the teachings of our Blessed Lord and Saviour ... in the practice of his doctrine today is instilled the propaganda that seeks to make the race that you and I represent an inferior unit of the great human family." **(End)**

"... the records will show ... that I have always been a Christian and was confirmed by the Catholic Bishop who testified on my behalf." **(End)**

"You have come into our homes, deceived us in every way under the guise of Christianity - but do not you ever believe that I am not a Christian. I believe in God the Father, God the Son and God the Holy Ghost; I endorse the Nicene creed; I believe that Jesus died for me; I believe that God lives for me and for all men; and no condition that you can impose on me by deceiving me about Christianity will cause me to doubt Jesus Christ and to doubt God. I shall never hold Christ or God responsible for the commercialisation of Christianity by heartless men who adopt it as the easiest means of fooling and robbing other people out of their land and country." **(End)**

"Christ was God in the perfect sense of the mind and soul. His spirit was truly God's spirit ... Christ never disobeyed the holy spirit of goodness, and that was why he was the Son of man with whom the spirit of God was well pleased because he lived a life so perfect as was intended when God made Adam and Eve. The mission of Christ, therefore was to redeem man from sin and place him back on the pinnacle of goodness as God intended ..." **(End)**

"Man was redeemed by Christ to reach the perfect state as man, through his soul ... The shortest prayer we may give to God, even if we never pray otherwise, is to make the sign of the cross, and say at the same time, 'In the name of the Father, the Son and the Holy Ghost'." **(End)**

"No man has ever seen God. Suppose you, like Christ, could see God." **(End)**.

7.3.2 Managing religion for unity

"Man's religion is something that we cannot eliminate from his system or destroy in him, therefore it is folly for any man to go about attacking another man's religion, because to him it is fundamental". **(End)**.

"... any man who gets out and attacks religions, thinking he can convert men to the organisation by doing so is not helping the organisation. He is doing more harm than good." **(End)**.

"God tells us to worship him in our own image. We are black and to be in our own image, God must be black." **(End)**.

"The only cause that held us together as a people was RELIGION. During the days of slavery religion was the only consolation for the [Afrikan], and then it was given to him by his masters. Immediately after the emancipation, when the [Afrikan] was thrown back on his own resources, the illiterate race preacher took charge of us, and with the eye of selfishness he exploited the zeal of the religious." **(End)**.

7.3.3 Religion as the oppressor's tool

"I am not responsible, neither is any other [Afrikan person], for the accident of birth in the western world, for we are all relics of slavery, an institution that was forced upon our fathers and made justified in the name of Christianity ..." **(End)**.

"No two persons think alike, even if they outwardly profess the same faith ..." **(End)**.

"... whilst we are hoping by our Christian virtues to have an entry into paradise we also realise that we are living on earth, and that the things that are practiced in paradise are not practiced here. You have to treat the world as the world treats you; we are living in a temporal material age, an age of activity, an age of racial, national selfishness. What else can you expect but to give back to the world what the world gives to you ..." **(End)**.

"... God had nothing to do with the campaign of Italy in Abyssinia, for on the one side we had the Pope of the Catholic Church blessing the crusade, and on the other, the Coptic Church fasting and praying with confidence of victory ... the Italians triumphed by the use of mustard Gas. It is logical therefore that God did not take sides, but left the matter to be settled by the strongest human battalion." **(End)**

"We are not going to get it [freedom] by worrying God about it, because HE is not a political agent of anybody ... God has given you the character to get anything you want without playing God ..." **(End)** [and in any event] "... the power that holds Afrika is not divine" **(End)**.

"... selected the job to save the body as the soul, and if God didn't intend that, he never would have made man with a body." **(End)**.

7.4 In defence of the organisation
7.4.1 Enemy within (the organisation)

"Always try to pacify, always bring factions together in keeping with the principles of the association. Always try to compromise the factions towards keeping the peace." **(End)**

"But, men, remember this. You at this time can only be destroyed by yourselves, from within and not from without. You have reached the point where the victory is to be won from within and can only be lost from within." **(End)**

"We must realise that our greatest enemi[es] are not those on the outside, but those in our midst's, because when we can readily recognise the enemies on the outside and do not allow them to pass, we have those on the inside working with us to destroy us without our knowing." **(End)**

"Traitors are working hard, the enemies are doing their worst; but we smile in their faces. There are combinations of forces working against the UNIA, against which it is written by these enemies, 'The association and Garvey must be destroyed.' They have been using men once placed in positions of trust in this association to help destroy the movement. These traitors we have had to dismiss. Today they, with the rest of our enemies, are determined to tear down the structure that we have built. They have all entered into a conspiracy to sue and embarrass the UNIA … these traitors are endeavouring to embarrass us before the courts, suing us for salaries, trying to force judgements upon us at a time when we are supposed to be fighting the common enemy, so that they could glory in the downfall of the movement." **(End)**

"The fools who condemn a movement like this are without sense, are without brains! But, men, let me tell you, they are not such fools after all. They are the paid agents of the ancient enemy, to cut you off from the vision that you have husbanded. They are the paid agents of the enemy to disrupt you in this hour of world readjustment. If these ancient enemies of ours obstruct the vision of 400,000,000 [Afrikan people] for a while, they will be able ultimately to completely control Afrika, and once and for all seal the doom of this race of ours." **(End)**

"In [US Satan] and the West Indies, we have [Afrikans] who believe themselves so much above their fellows as to cause them to think that any readjustment in the affairs of the race should be placed in their hands for them to exercise a kind of an autocratic and despotic control as others have done to us for centuries." **(End)**

"… as far as the UNIA is concerned, I have no friends. I have no brother, I have no sister, I have no father, I have no wife where the UNIA is concerned. When it comes to my life outside, I have my friends. If you want a dollar and I have two, I will slip you one. But if it comes to the UNIA, and you have taken a dollar and I know it, you are going to jail, as far as Marcus Garvey is concerned. And when you are gone to jail, as your personal friend I will feel sorry for you and try to get a bond man to take you out of jail, but first of all, I will have done my duty to the UNIA, to the post I hold, to the people and to my God. If you are dishonest and you know it now, clear out of this Convention, because you are going to be exposed. There is nothing to be covered here. We are going to expose everybody who has something to expose." **(End)**

"RD Jonas the man implicated in the Chicago riot is an imposter who uses the name of the Black Star Line and the UNIA to extract money from [Afrikan people]. He has no connection with these corporations. He and Redding are frauds. Deal with them according to the law. They are unworthy of sympathy." **(End)**

7.4.2 Enemy within (the race)

"We have unscrupulous men and organizations working in opposition to us. Some trying to capitalize the new spirit that has come to the [Afrikan] to make profit out of it to their own selfish benefit; some are trying to set back the [Afrikan] from seeing the hope of his own liberty, and thereby poisoning our people's mind against the motives of our organization; but every sensible far-seeing [Afrikan] in this enlightened age knows what propaganda means. It is the medium of discrediting that which you are opposed to, so that the propaganda of our enemies will be of little avail as soon as we are rendered able to carry to our peoples scattered throughout the world the true message of our great organisation." **(End)**

"... my rivals and enemies tried to use the honourable court and the prospective jurors of Jewish and Catholic origin and faith in prejudice against me, by circulating before and during the trial thousands of printed circulars and letters wickedly and viciously stating that I was a member of the Ku Klux Klan and against all Jews and Catholics; hence they should send me to prison because Catholics and Jews were judges, district attorneys, jurors and policemen." **(End)**.

7.4.3 Enemy without

"... it is on the same principle of injustice that England exploits Afrika, that France exploits Afrika, that Italy exploits Afrika, that Belgium exploits Afrika, that the stronger nations of the world exploit the weak." **(End)**

"We are going to show them the quality of mercy – after we get even with the 'crackers.' I don't believe there can be any dispensation of mercy until we 'get even' with the 'other fellow.' I believe in the 'eye for an eye' principle, and the 'tooth for a tooth' Business; I believe in that religion, and I believe in showing the other fellow mercy – after I 'get even' with him; only then. I want to be satisfied that he feels what I felt, and then, after that, we can call it quits, for we can appreciate each other's feelings." **(End)**

"Propaganda can be true or false in its origin or intent; but it is always directed at the public for the purpose of winning the support of the public to the sentiment expressed in the propaganda. If you hate a man, giving him a bad name might well explain one of the purposes of propaganda without truth behind it ... Don't follow the band down the street because it plays sweet music to the propaganda of the circus manager. He may lead you into the circus tent and take away your pocket book; that is to say, don't get on anybody's bandwagon, because he may drive you to hell with his sweet music. Like the Pied Piper of Hamlin, who played his sweet pipe and led the rats out of the city and into the sea and drowned them.

Propaganda organised by somebody else, is always calculated to take advantage of you. Don't help them do so. Always ask, what is this about? What is the object of this? Who has sent this out? What is he aiming at? Will it hurt me and my race? Is he trying to get an advantage over me? Is it honest? Is it true? If you ask these questions of all propaganda that comes up, before you swallow it, you will be able to take care of yourself." **(End)**

"Propaganda is a method used by organised peoples to convert others to their will.

We of the [Afrikan] race are suffering more than any other race in the world from propaganda – Propaganda to destroy our hopes, our ambitions and our self confidence." **(End)**

"The only protection against INJUSTICE in man is POWER – [legal,] physical, financial and scientific." **(End)**

7.4.4 Counter attack

"Divide your enemies so as to gain your advantage. Always keep them divided so as to be able to gain the advantage. Your only hope of escaping the hate and prejudice of other people is to keep them severely occupied with other problems. If they have nothing else to attend to, they will concentrate on you and your problems will be aggravated." **(End)**

Pan-Afrikanism: From Programme to Philosophy

Strategically selected quotes from Marcus Garvey

8 Organisational relations with outsiders

8.1 Afrikan people are our primary concern

"Men, there is much to live for, and there is much to die for. The man, the race o[r] nation that is not prepared to risk life itself for the possession of an ideal, shall lose that ideal. If you, I repeat, must be free, you yourselves must strike the blow. I am not speaking of any other freedom than Afrikan freedom because other men are capable of advocating their own causes." **(End)**

"I have respect for every race. I believe the Irish should be free; they should have a country. I believe the Jew should be free and the Egyptian should be free, and the Indian and the Poles. I believe also that the Black man should be free. I would fight for the freedom of the

Jew, the Irish, the Poles; I would fight and die for the liberation of 400,000,000 [Afrikans]." **(End)**

8.2 Building alliances

"Understand, we recognize humanity; we love humanity, and we are about to bring about an alliance with all humanity, that is as far as that section and portion of humanity will ally itself with us." **(End)**

"We must call an alliance because we have been too careless with ourselves in the past. The New [Afrikan] is going to form an alliance somewhere. We have no objection to forming an alliance with white people; we are willing to form it now, but in forming that alliance we say: what is good for you is good for us too. That is the principle of our alliance, and listen, you cannot ignore us because we are 400 million strong." **(End)**

"We are willing to form an alliance with the great white race for the preservation of civilisation, and for the good of a lasting peace, but it must be clearly understood that the New [Afrikan] is quite a different man from the [Afrikan] of seven or eight years ago. Universally we stand on the platform of human justice, human rights and human liberty. We are not going to yield one bit on these great principles. Men have fought for them, they have died for them in the past and we are willing to fight to see Afrika restored to us as our home." **(End)**

8.3 Acts of solidarity

"I have to thank my white friends and members of my organisation ... who helped generally in my being admitted to bail." **(End)**.

"I succeeded to a great extent in establishing the association in Jamaica with the assistance of a Catholic Bishop, the Governor, Sir John Pringle, the Reverend William Graham, a Scottish clergy man, and several other white friends." **(End)**.

"... I can say that some of the most influential of them [Europeans] have paid us the honour of coming among us. His Excellency the Governor, the Colonial Secretary, Hon. H. Bryan, C.M.G., Sir John Pringle, Hon.

Brigadier-General, L.S. Blackden, all members of the privy council, have been our patrons on several occasions and they are still friends of the association. The Brigadier-General has lectured to us, also his Lordship Bishop J.J. Collins, S.J., His Worship the Mayor of Kingston, Hon H.A.L. Simpson, M.L.C., Mr. R.W. Bryant, J.P., ex-Mayor of Kingston who has visited us on more than a dozen times, and many other prominent dignitaries in the country. The Hon. Colonial Secretary has himself attended a function along with his wife to which he was specifically invited." **(End)**.

"I unhesitatingly endorse the race purity idea of Mr Powell and his organisation, and I have pledged my moral support to their program expecting of the honourable and honest of this race the regard and support for ours ... I am asking you, my friends and co-workers, to hear Mr Powell, whom I have invited to speak to you. Extend to him and the Anglo-Saxon Clubs the courtesy and fellowship that is logical to the program of the Universal Improvement Association." **(End)**

8.4 Attitude towards non-Afrikans

"The UNIA stands for Human rights, not only [Afrikan] rights, but for all races. The UNIA believes in not only the rights of the [Afrikan] race, but the white race, the yellow race and the brown race." **(End)**

"This is an age that is causing all men to feel that they are entitled to liberty and freedom. We are not selfish in our desire for freedom. We know that there are many other peoples that are suffering just as we are suffering. We are in sympathy with the great Irish people who have been overrun for the last 700 years by the tyrants of ... Britain; we are in sympathy with the people of India, with a population of 380,000,000 who are dominated by ... Britain. We are in sympathy with the Chinese, the Egyptians but one and all we are in sympathy with ourselves, and we shall so unite our forces that within the next decade we shall find ourselves a free people and a great people, too." **(End)**

"We are not preaching a propaganda of hate against anybody. We love the white man; we love all humanity, because we feel that we cannot live without the other. The white man is as necessary to the existence of the [Afrikan] as the [Afrikan] is as necessary to his existence. There is a common relationship that we cannot escape. Afrika has certain things that Europe wants, and Europe has certain things that Afrika wants, and if a fair and square deal must bring white and black with each other, it is impossible for us to escape it. Afrika has oil, diamonds, copper, gold and rubber and all the minerals that Europe wants, and there must be some kind of relationship between Afrika and Europe for a fair exchange, so we cannot afford to hate anybody." **(End)**

"The UNIA believes in the fellowship of races. We have a high regard for the white race; we have a high regard for all other races of the world; but we believe in the Golden rule and its application to all races: 'Do unto others as you would that they to you should do.' When the white race, and the yellow race, and all other races are willing to do to the [Afrikan] as the [Afrikan] is willing to do unto them, then we shall have the reign of peace ..." **(End)**

"We must learn to give and take, if we want Afrika, as we surely do, we must reasonably make up our minds to yield some things and make concessions in [US Satan] and other white countries by sane and proper arrangements ... what does the [Afrikan] want? Afrika for those at home and abroad, for it is our only hope and salvation; other than this the race is lost ..." **(End)**

"... we must get the co-operation and sympathy of our white brothers ..." **(End)**

"... up to now my one true friend as far as you can rely on his friendship is the white man." **(End)**

8.5 On Lenin

"... probably the greatest man in the world between 1917 and the hour of 1924 when he breathed his last and took his flight from this world ... The class of the exploiter and robber looked upon him as a revolutionist and a menace to society. That class is glad that Lenin is dead. But as they rejoice over the death of **this great man,** so the millions of the peasantry in Russia **and the millions of the oppressed people of the world** bow their heads in solemn reverence, in sorrow and condolence over the loss of this great man ... And we also, as [Afrikan people], mourn for Lenin. Not one but the 400,000,000's of us should mourn over the death of this great man, because Russia promised great hope not only to [Afrikan people] but to the weaker peoples of the world ... We mourn with the proletariat of the world for the demise of the world's greatest leader ..." **(End)**

"... Russia through her social democratic system promised a revolution to the world that would truly and indeed emancipate the souls of men everywhere. [Afrikan people] have not yet gotten to realise the effect of certain world changes. We of the UNIA who lead have studied carefully and keenly the activities of Lenin and Trotsky ... we of the UNIA, as I said, had our opinion, had our own idea in the matter of the new government of Russia. And it is without any hesitancy, without any reserve, we could not but favour the existence of a social democratic government in Russia or in any other part of the world, because we are of the class that rules in Russia and naturally our sympathy should be with the people who feel with us, who suffer with us ... I believe, in time, that the whole world will take on the social democratic system now existing in Russia." **(End)**

"... We are not Russians. We are [Afrikan people]. But we can learn lessons from this. It is the lesson that Russia teaches us that interests me, the lesson wherein the majority of the people are able to rule, to establish a government. All majorities should rule. And that is why we suffer so in this country, because the majority rule. The majority will always rule. The majority should always rule. And it is because we realise our impotence as minorities scattered here and there that we are endeavouring to link these minorities into a great majority, that we also may rule." **(End)**

"... I trust that when you read things said about Lenin you will be able to have your own opinion and form your own conclusion. The average [Afrikan person] is lead away by what he reads, he is led away by what he hears. You do not always read the best of the individual. You do not always hear the best of individuals, and it is rather unsafe for anyone to form an opinion just by what he has read or just by what he has seen or heard. Opinion should be formed only after most careful examination of the truth ... You are not to form your opinion about men and about measures just by what you read or by what you hear, but you must place yourself in the position mentally where you are able to discriminate until you have found the truth, then you will go and pass your opinion on the truth ... A lot of unkind things are said of the world's greatest leaders and benefactors. But if we were to form our opinion about leaders and individuals who are probably before the public on the strength of just what is written and what is said, we today would have very few leaders, because very few men would be bold enough to be leaders." **(End)**

8.6 Separatism as a tactic

"I calculated when I started this movement that we would have worked together and kept our own counsel as a race of people without mixing much with other folks, without going to other folks, and I was successful in keeping to that policy up to three months ago. I calculated that not until the proper time had we to approach the other fellow and tell him what we wanted. That time naturally would come. We could not do everything on this side of the Atlantic without ultimately telling the white man what we want. But I believed the time had not come yet. I do not believe in doing anything prematurely, and I calculated that we would have just worked among ourselves until we were ready and then gone to the other fellow and said, 'we are ready, and we are asking you to let us come to terms and get this thing done.' But, apparently, some of our folks are forcing us to talk with the other fellow before the time comes." **(End)**

8.7 Excluding non-Afrikans from meetings

"... Liberty hall welcomes all friends of liberty. We welcome the Irish, we welcome the Jews, the Egyptians, the Hindus, and all people struggling for liberty, because we are in sympathy with suffering humanity everywhere ... we are in sympathy with the cause of freedom everywhere ... we welcome this friend of Soviet Russia [Rose Pastor Stokes] to tell us a little about what her people are doing to get liberty, and if we can find any good in what she says we shall certainly be quick to seize upon it and adopt it for our own benefit..." **(End)**.

"I trust there is no prejudiced white man in this building. I trust all the white people in this building will enter into the spirit of this meeting as if it were a white meeting, and as a white man speaking to white people in the interests of white people." **(End)**

"... I am asking you, my friends and co-workers, to hear Mr Powell, whom I have invited to speak to you." **(End)**.

"Contributions to the UNIA should generally be accepted from [Afrikans], but where other people of other races can be approached and are willing to give help, such help may be accepted, but without any strings attached or promises made that would in any way compromise the clear cut intelligence of the policy of the UNIA. *Such contributions do not entitle the donors to any privileges of membership or any right to attend meetings of the UNIA, except public meetings as guests.* Their contribution should never entitle them to take part in any business meetings of the organisation. Their donations may be accepted in the same way as [Afrikans] give to white organisations; without having any claim on those organisations." **(End)**

Strategically selected quotes from Marcus Garvey

9 Reparations and Repatriation

9.1 Reparations

"I am here this evening as the President General of the UNIA, an organisation of 11 million [Afrikan people] in Afrika, [US Satan], South America, Central America, Canada and the West Indies to present to you the claim of our race upon your civilisation." **(End)**

"We once had civilisation and we got tired of it, and we called in the white man and gave it to him, and he has been keeping and using it for us for several hundred years, but we have just changed our minds now. We ask and demand a part of that civilisation for ourselves. We are not going to be unfair about it; we are not going to collect any interest." **(End)**

"A year ago Senator MacCullum of the Mississippi Legislature introduced a resolution in the House for the purpose of petitioning the Congress of [US Satan] and the President to use their good influence in securing from the Allies sufficient territory in Afrika in liquidation of the war debt, which territory should be used for the establishing of an independent nation for American [Afrikans]. About the same time Senator France of Maryland gave expression to a similar desire in the Senate of [US Satan]. During a speech on the 'Soldiers' Bonus.' He said: 'We owe a big debt to Afrika and one which we have too long ignored. I need not enlarge upon our peculiar interest in the obligation to the people of Afrika. Thousands of Americans have for years been contributing to the missionary work which has been carried out by the noble men and women who have been sent out in that field by the churches of America.'

This reveals a real change on the part of prominent statesmen in their attitude on the Afrikan question. Then comes another suggestion from Germany, for which Dr. Heinrich Schnee, a former Governor of German East Afrika, is author ... that America takes over the mandatories of Great Britain and France in Afrika for the colonization of American [Afrikans]. Speaking on the matter, he says 'As regards the attempt to colonize Afrika with the surplus American coloured population, this would in a long way settle the vexed problem, and under the plan such as Senator France has outlined, might enable France and Great Britain to discharge their duties to the [US Satan], and simultaneously ease the burden of German reparations which is paralyzing economic life.' With expressions as above quoted from prominent world statesmen, and from the demands made by such men as Senators France and McCullum, it is clear that the question of Afrikan nationality is not a far-fetched one, but is as reasonable and feasible as was the idea of an American nationality." **(End)**

"After the white man is through abusing the [Afrikan], when he gets back his sober senses, he will realise that he owes all he possesses today to the [Afrikan]. The [Afrikan] gave him science and art and literature and everything that is dear to him today, and the white man has kept them for thousands of years, and he has taken advantage of the world. He has even gone out of his way to reduce the Afrikan that gave him civilisation and kept him as a slave for two hundred years and fifty years. But we feel the time has come when we must take hold of that civilisation that we once held. The hour has struck for the [Afrikan] to be once more a power in the world, and not all white men in the world will be able to hold the [Afrikan] from becoming a power in the next century. Not even the powers of hell will be able to stop the [Afrikan] in the onward and upward movement." **(End)**

9.2 Repatriation

"Understand this Afrikan programme well. I am not saying that all [Afrikans] of [US Satan] should go to Afrika; I am not saying that all the [Afrikans] in the West Indies should go back to Afrika, but I say this: That some serious attempt must be made to build up a government and a nation strong [enough] to protect the [Afrikan] or your future in [US Satan] will not be worth a snap of the finger. There are many of us here who cannot and will not go back to Afrika because of property interests or because of certain conditions, climactic or otherwise. But we are saying that Afrika still is your only hope; that without an independent Afrika – without a powerful Afrika you are lost." **(End)**

"It is a mistake to suppose that I want to take the [Afrikans] to Afrika. I believe that the American [Afrikans] have helped to establish North American civilisation and, therefore, have a perfect right to live in [US Satan] and to aspire to equal opportunities and treatment. Each [Afrikan] can be a citizen of the nation in which he was born or that he has chosen. But I foresee the building of a great state in Afrika which, featuring in the concert of great nations, will make the [Afrikan] race as respectable as the others ... Cuban [Afrikans] will be favoured by the building of this Afrikan state because when this state exists they will be considered and respected as descendents of this powerful country which has enough strength to protect them." **(End)**

"The people who live in Liberia today are blood of our blood and flesh of our flesh, especially the ruling element, the Americo-West Indian Liberians. They represent in Liberia today the off-spring of an earlier generation of [Afrikan people] who went from this country and from the West Indies one hundred years ago, eighty years ago, fifty years ago, one-quarter of a century ago to make it possible to find and have freedom, a freedom that would, indeed, be worthwhile not only for themselves, but for the rest of their kind." **(End)**

"... between January 1 and December 31, 1921, it is expected that the UNIA and the Black Star Line will have transported between five hundred thousand and one million civilised, industrious [Afrikans] from the western hemisphere to the great Republic of Liberia." **(End)**

"We are asking the world for a fair chance. That is all we ask for. We are asking the world for a fair chance to assist the people of Liberia in developing that country, as the world is giving the Jew a fair chance to develop Palestine. And, if they do not give us a fair chance, we are going to raise hell." **(End)**

"Several people have charged us with an intention of entering Afrika at a certain place that is known for the purpose of creating a disturbance in Afrika. They charge us with desiring to convert Liberia into a battle ground. I deny any such intention on the part of the UNIA. I desire to let the world know that we recognise not only Liberia as belonging to the [Afrikan], but all Afrika. And since Liberia is already occupied by Afrikans we have no need to make entry through Liberia, but we shall make our entry wheresoever we place our feet in Afrika. Whether we land in the South or the West or the North or in Central Afrika there shall be the battleground for Afrikan freedom. And it does not mean that American [Afrikans] are going to do it. It will be done in Afrika even without our going there." **(End)**

"In the forward step to establish colonies in Afrika, the association sent a delegation to the League of nations at Geneva, in 1922, to present to that body a petition asking for the turning over to the organisation all of the late German Afrikan colonies, which were taken from them during the war by black soldiers, and which were claimed by France and England." **(End)**

"Of course we'll have to kick the Europeans out of Afrika. You would like to know by what means we are going to carry out this task. Allow me not to speak for I would let out a secret of this organisation." **(End)**

"In keeping with the Fourteenth article of the petition, Your Excellencies are hereby informed that the delegation from the Third Annual International Convention of the [Afrikan] people of the world will wait upon the Assembly during its entire session from 4th September, to be available for personally presenting the claims of the [Afrikan] race, and to answer all the questions that may be submitted by the League. It is felt that the delegation will be given the consideration merited because of the importance of the representation.

Your excellencies are hereby informed, that the Third Annual International Convention of the [Afrikan] peoples of the world is a duly elected body representing the interests of the four hundred million [Afrikans] of the world, and that the accompanying petition is an expression of the feeling of the [Afrikan] race." **(End)**

"At Versailles when the Peace Treaty was to be signed you called everybody in and you distributed the spoils of war to everybody. You gave the Jew, Palestine; you gave the Egyptians a larger modicum of self-government; you gave the Irish Home Rule government and Dominion status; you gave the poles a new government of their own. But what did you give the [Afrikan]? What did you do to the [Afrikan]? You threw his dead body on the streets of Cardiff, smashed the coffin and kicked the corpse about and made a football of it after he came back from the war." **(End)**

"[Afrikan people in Kenya] stopped all public vehicles, and told those white robbers riding in them to get out and walk! Now, that shows some new spirit, anyhow – stopped every buggy, stopped every carriage that went by, and told the occupants to get out and walk. That shows that they are coming, doesn't it. The only handicap they had, was that they had sticks and stones. Now it is for you men and women who are mixed up with modern civilisation for three hundred years to give them something else besides sticks and stones. You have to give them the latest output of science. I won't tell you wha[t] it is. It means that you and I must get busy now, because all the Afrikans now have are sticks and stones, and they cannot do anything with such weapons or means of defence." **(End)**

"It will not be to go to Afrika for the purpose of exercising an overlordship over the natives, but it shall be the purpose of the UNIA to have established in Afrika that brotherly co-operation which will make the interests of the Afrikan native and the American and West Indian [Afrikan] one and the same, that is to say, we shall enter into a common partnership to build up Afrika in the interests of our race. **(End)**

Strategically selected quotes from Marcus Garvey

10 Measures of Achievement

10.1 Organisational

"... in our desire to lift ourselves to that standard we shall stop at nothing until there is a free and redeemed Afrika ... we who make up this Organization know no turning back, we have pledged ourselves even unto the last drop of our sacred blood that Afrika must be free ... I prefer to die at this moment rather than not to work for the freedom of Afrika ... It falls to our lot to tear off the shackles that bind Mother Afrika. Can you do it? You did it in the Revolutionary War. You did it in the Civil War; You did it in the Battles of Marne and Verdun; You did it in Mesopotamia. You can do it marching up the battle heights of Afrika. Let the world know that 400,000,000 [Afrikans] are prepared to die or live as free men." **(End)**

"Four years ago, realizing the oppression and the hardships from which we suffered, we organized ourselves into an organisation for the purpose of bettering our condition, and founding a government of our own. The four years of organization have brought good results, in that from obscure, despised race we have grown into a mighty power, a mighty force whose influence is being felt throughout the length and breadth of the world." **(End)**

"And if our work of the last 15 years was to be measured by profits and dividends, we could fairly say that the UNIA has been the most successful movement not only among [Afrikans] but among all races during that period of time. The dividends that we have paid are that we have stirred Afrika from centre to circumference. In every section of our homeland, the [Afrikan] is now awakened through our propaganda of 'Afrika for the Afrikans, at home and abroad.'" **(End)**

"... our organisation is recognised as a world power, and appreciated not only by ourselves but by established governments of the world ..." **(End)**

10.2 Personal

"Marcus Garvey, when he dies, will not die alone; when Marcus Garvey dies for the principles of the UNIA, mark well. Before Garvey goes, Garvey shall have laid a foundation for other Garveys who will be more deadly in their sting than the one who passes off ... for Garvey is but laying the cornerstone for the incoming of the New Afrika ..." **(End)**

"... though an Englishman may treat my words with levity and think I am a fool, as newspapers like the *Daily Sketch* tried to make out, you will find ten years from now, or 100 years from now, Garvey was not an idle buffoon but was representing a new vision of the [Afrikan] who was looking forward to great accomplishments in the future." **(End)**

"My success as a[n] organiser was much more than my rival [Afrikan] leaders could tolerate. They, regardless of the consequences, either to me, or to the race, had to destroy me by fair means or fowl. Thousands of anonymous and other hostile letters written to editors and publishers of the white press by [Afrikan] rivals to prejudice me in the eyes of public opinion are sufficient evidence of the wicked and vicious opposition I have had to meet from among my own people, especially among the very light coloured. But they went further than the press in their attempts to discredit me. They organised clubs all over [US Satan] and the West Indies, and wrote both open and anonymous letters to city, State and Federal officials of this and other Governments to induce them to use their influence to hamper and destroy me. No wonder, therefore, that several Judges, District Attorneys and other high officials have been against me without knowing me." **(End)**

Strategically selected quotes from Marcus Garvey

11 Contextual issues

11.1 The central Importance of Afrika

"Afrika is the only hope because you cannot claim your rights anywhere else except that you claim it by force of strength and governmental protection. You cannot claim it from [US Satan], because there can be but one government in [US Satan] and that shall always be a white man's government. The white man will only respect your rights constitutionally as a citizen of the country or as a resident of the country, when you have some government behind you. When You can compel a nation to respect your rights because of your connection with some government that is sufficiently strong to support you, then and only then will you be respected." **(End)**

"We were misinformed about Afrika for three hundred years. But in 1919 the New [Afrikan] is not misinformed about Afrika. He is well informed about Afrika, and he knows that Afrika is the richest continent in the world. He knows that Afrika is the bone of contention between white men and yellow men. He knows that the fight between ... Britain and Germany was a fight for Afrikan aggrandisement. Up to now the Kaiser would have been giving them trouble if it were not for the [Afrikan] ... we have defeated the Kaiser and have given victory to the allies, England, France and Italy, but we are not through with the war because we intend to take Afrika for four hundred million Black folks of the world ... England has been living as a parasite on the great continent of Afrika, but today every Black man intends to pick on the parasite and throw the parasite away. We say if Afrika is good enough to build up England, if Afrika is good enough to build up France, if Afrika is good enough to build up Italy and build up Belgium, the Belgium of Leopold of the Congo, then Afrika ought to be good enough for finding a home and a place in the sun for the Black Ethiopians scattered all over the world." **(End)**

"England wants money, France wants money, Italy wants money, Belgium wants money, Portugal and Spain want money, and the only place they can grind it from today is Afrika; hence, they are making one mad determination to exploit and ravage that country, the land of our fathers, without any consideration for humanity or Christian fellowship. If they profess other than their lust for gold, then we know it is a lie; it is all a farce, pretence, hypocrisy." **(End)**

"The Afrika that they have taught us of fifty years ago, of eighty years ago, a hundred years ago, as being a hideous place to live in, a place to be avoided, is the Afrika that has been parcelled out North, South, East and West. It is the Afrika that caused the bloody war of 1914, and it is the Afrika that is going to cause another bloody war." **(End)**

"We are aggrieved because of this partitioning of Afrika, because it seeks to deprive [Afrikans] of the chance of a higher national development; no chance, no opportunity, is given to us to prove our fitness to govern, to dominate on our own behalf. They impute so many bad things against Haiti and against Liberia so as to make it impossible for us to demonstrate our ability for self-government." **(End)**

"... we of the UNIA have a programme of constructive government for Afrika, the Afrika from which we were robbed 300 years ago – as I said awhile ago – is the Afrika, the motherland, the fatherland, that is calling us today, and the country that will save us tomorrow. Without Afrika the [Afrikans] in all parts of the world are doomed." **(End)**

"All that we want is that each and everyone will entre the fold of this great and noble organisation and let us unitedly march to our destiny. Turn your attention not away from Afrika, because Afrika shall be the only salvation and solution of this great problem of race in [US Satan] and in the world. Afrika, the land of our fathers, beckons us home, if not in person, in sympathy, in sentiment and in moral and financial help, so why shouldn't we help her to throw of the shackles place upon her by an alien civilisation and alien races?" **(End)**

"... the best thing for every one to do, is to unite, and so fortify ourselves by building up a strong Government in Afrika, that as citizens of that government, we can claim protection in any part of the world we happen to find ourselves. Why should not Afrika have a Navy? Why should not Afrika have a standing Army? Why should not Afrika have a government second to none in the world, controlled and dominated by [Afrikan people]?" **(End)**

"The [Afrikan] must have a country and a nation of his own." **(End)**.

"Let Afrika be your guiding star – our star of destiny." **(End)**)

"Afrikan for the Afrikans" **(End)**.

"If Black men have no right in [US Satan]; if black men have no right in Canada; if Black men have no right in Australia; if Black men have no right in England; if Black men have no right in France; if black men have no right in Italy, white men shall have no right in Afrika." **(End)**

"Remember we did not sell Afrika – we were taken away from there three hundred years ago." **(End)**

"Afrika must be for the Afrikans, and for them exclusively" **(End)**

"... the UNIA wants to make Afrika absolutely a Black man's country."

(End)

11.2 The critically important impact of World War I

"The war helped a great deal in arousing the consciousness of [Afrikan] people to the reasonableness of our programme, especially after the British at home had rejected a large number of West Indian coloured men who wanted to be officers in the British army." **(End)**

"The war of 1914-1918 has created a new sentiment throughout the world. Once upon a time weaker peoples were afraid of expressing themselves, of giving vent to their feelings, but today no oppressed race, no oppressed nation is afraid of speaking out in the cause of liberty." **(End)**

"We are a new people, born out of a new day and a new circumstance. We are born out of the bloody wa[r] of 1914-18. A new spirit, a new courage, has come to us simultaneously as it came to the other peoples of the world. It came to us at the same time it came to the Jew. When the Jew said, 'We shall have Palestine!' the same sentiment came to us when we said, 'We shall have Afrika!' Therefore the purpose that reveals why we have allies all around the colours of the UNIA all over the world until we are three and a half million strong, and on the first of August the representatives of the three and a half millions and the representatives of the 400,000,000 of the race will assemble themselves at Liberty Hall to write to the Magna Carta of our liberty and our rights." **(End)**

"We speak tonight, not in the spirit of cowardice, but as men who died in France in 1914-1918, and since we could have died in France we can now die right here." **(End)**

"Out of this war we have produced the American, or the West Indian, or the Afrikan Napoleon who will ultimately lead the 400,000,000 Black people of the world to victory." **(End)**

"We New [Afrikan people in US Satan] declare that we desire liberty or will take death. They called us out but a few months ago to fight three thousand miles away in Europe to save civilisation, to give liberty and democracy to other peoples of the world. And we fought so splendidly, and after we died, after we gave up our blood, and some of us survived and returned to our respective countries, in [US Satan], in the West Indies, in Central America and in Afrika, they told us, as they told us in the past, that this country is the white man's country." **(End)**

"... thousands of [Afrikans] out of 2,000,000 called, died on the battle fields of France and Flanders. We died there gladly, thinking that we are shedding our blood for a real cause. After the blood is shed we now realise that it was farcical cause; that we have found out our mistake before it is too late; we say we shall continue the war until we get democracy ... we fought, and after the battle what was done to us? They mobbed us in Liverpool, in London and Manchester. The English in Wales stopped the funeral procession of the West Indian [Afrikan], smashed the coffin, cut off the head of the dead man and made a football of it." **(End)**

"Our Fatherland, Afrika, is bleeding, and she is now stretching forth her hands to her children in [US Satan], the West Indies and Central America and Canada to help her. We must help her, therefore I hereby ask every [Afrikan] in the world to get ready for the next World War, twenty, thirty, thirty or forty years hence. The next World War shall find [Afrikans] fighting together to free our common Fatherland. Now it is no time for the [Afrikan] to be divided between two opinions. We must be pro-[Afrikan], and without offence to any one." **(End)**

"Must organise to know what we are to get out of the next war and see that we get it before one sacrifice is made." **(End)**

"Wherever you be today, in America, Afrika, Canada, the West Indies, South or Central America, let your cry be 'liberty or death.' Prepare your minds, your hearts and your swords for the next World war. It will come whether it is to be between Asia and Europe, or Europe and Afrika, be assured that it will come, and at the time we hope every Black man will be ready to take of himself.

Fight the good fight therefore, and be always in readiness for the bugle call of Mother Afrika." **(End)**

"If the war had continued for two weeks longer I would have had to go to France and Flanders to die for the Belgian. According to the law I would have been compelled to go. I know there are going to be more wars within the next 25 years, and [Afrikans] will be called upon." **(End)**

"There can be no peace among men and nations, so long as the strong continue to oppress the weak, so long as injustice is done to other peoples, just so long will we have cause for war, and make a lasting peace an impossibility." **(End)**

"There will be no peace in the world until the white man confines himself politically to Europe, the yellow man to Asia and the Black man to Afrika. The original division of the earth among mankind must stand, and any one who dares to interfere with this division creates only trouble for himself." **(End)**

11.3 Revolution

"I beseech you, men and women of the race, to steal your hearts, your minds and your souls for the coming conflict of ideals. The whole world is in turmoil and the revolution threatens. Asia and Europe are preparing for this revolution. It will mean the survival of the fittest, and I now declare that Afrika must also prepare; for in the triumph of the forces of white, yellow or black men in this coming revolution will hang the destiny of the world.

Sons and daughters of Afrika, scattered though you may be, I implore you to prepare. Prepare in all ways to strengthen the hand of Mother Afrika. Our mother has been bleeding for centuries from the injuries inflicted upon her by a merciless foe. The call is for the physician to heal the wounds, and there can be no other physician than the dark hued son of the mother, and there can be no other nurse as tender and kind as the daughter of the afflicted mother.

Let us turn back in this determination of ours. Afrika must be redeemed, but before her redemption we have to prove to the world we are fit. The chance to make ourselves fit is now presented to every son and daughter of Afrika." **(End)**

11.4 Hints of armed Struggle

"God made each and every one of us in his own image. God almighty when he created us gave us a common right, a common heritage. My right, my heritage I shall demand and if anyone attempts or dares to intrude upon my rights I shall fight and die in defence of those rights ... we are going to die alongside with you on the Afrikan continent. Somebody is crazy if you think the New [Afrikan] is going to allow himself to be a slave perpetually. No Sir; the New [Afrikan] is a man; if he cannot live a man he prefers to die a man." **(End)**

"... you will realise that liberty and democracy are very expensive things, and you have to give life for it. And if we [Afrikans] think we can get all these things without shedding blood for them we are making a dreadful mistake. You are not going to get anything unless you organise to fight for it. There are some things you can fight for constitutionally, such as your political rights, your civic rights, but to get liberty you have to shed blood for it. And that is what the UNIA is preparing your minds for – to shed some blood so as to make your race a free and independent race. That blood we are not going to shed in Newport news, that blood we are not going to shed in [US Satan], because [US Satan] will not be big enough to hold the [Afrikan] when the [Afrikan] gets ready. But that blood we are preparing to shed one day on the Afrikan battlefield, because it is the determination of the New [Afrikan] to repossess himself of that country that God gave to his forefathers. Afrika is the richest continent in the world; it is the country that has given civilisation to mankind and has made the white man what he is." **(End)**

"We of the UNIA are advocating the right for Afrika to develop herself as a mighty nation and give to herself the same kind of a naval and military protecting us as the other races." **(End)**

"We are tired of being kicked about; we are tired of being tossed around. The hour has come for a definite decision and we are about to take the step of decision. In this convention assembled we would like the world to understand that the [Afrikan] is prepared to be as peaceful now as he has always been, but nobody knows that the [Afrikan] is preparing to demand the things that are his. Yield up the things belonging to the [Afrikan] and we will have everlasting peace and abiding peace. It may seem strange to hear the [Afrikan] talk in terms of war, but that is the only medium through which men can get salvation … war to me is the only medium through which man can seek redemption. Now understand me well. We are gathered as an international body not to start war in any country where government is already constituted, but we are organised the world over first of all to demand the things that are belonging to [Afrikans] in Afrika, and if you refuse them[,] what you get, please take … A compromising coward has never won anything yet, since the dawn of creation." **(End)**

"I can see him now in the Virginia legislature of 140 years ago when he stood up among his fellow legislators and said: 'I care not what others may say, but as for me, give me liberty or give me death.' Tonight, as representatives of 400,000,000 [Afrikans] of the world we re-echo the words of Patrick Henry, 'We care not what others may say, but as for us, give us liberty or give us death.'" **(End)**

"Garvey is not satisfied because Garvey is not given a fair chance. What is true of Garvey is true of 400,000,000 [Afrikans] the world over. The New [Afrikan] therefore demands a chance; we are not praying for a chance; we are demanding a chance and we are going to take a chance, and if needs be we are going to die taking a chance. We are the friends of humanity; we are the friends of civilisation; but we desire just this; we desire equality from humanity and civilisation. That is what divides the Old and the New [Afrikan]. So tonight when we are assembled in this second Annual Convention of the [Afrikan] peoples of the World we would like it clearly understood by races, by nations, by governments everywhere that our desire is not to ferment trouble in any country where we live as subjects and citizens, but our desire is to free and liberate ourselves on the great continent of Afrika." **(End)**

"Under the League of Nations when Afrika revolts [US Satan] will have to call upon [Afrikans] to fight [Afrikans], therefore the League of Nations must be defeated by every [Afrikan] in [US Satan], or it will mean that Afrika will have to fight the combined nations of the world." **(End)**

Pan-Afrikanism: From Programme to Philosophy

Index

, Queen Mother Moore, 19
Abyssinia, 56
Afrika, 14, 17, 18, 21, 24, 25, 26, 35, 36, 41, 42, 45, 46, 48, 50, 51, 56, 57, 59, 64, 66, 71, 72, 73, 74, 75, 76, 77, 78, 81, 82, 83, 84, 85, 86, 87, 88, 89
Afrika for the Afrikans, 21, 36, 41, 48, 78
Afrikan citizens, 50
Afrikan community, 13, 18, 21
Afrikan Diaspora, 17
Afrikan for the Afrikans, 83
Afrikan liberation struggle, 13
Afrikan Orthodox Church, 19
Afrikan people, 14, 15, 17, 18, 19, 21, 24, 25, 41, 44, 45, 46, 49, 50, 52, 57, 58, 63, 67, 71, 74, 76, 83, 85
Afrikan Society Community Forum (PASCF), 13
Afrikan women, 19, 20, 30
Afro-Americans, 50
alliance, 64
American, 25, 26, 35, 72, 73, 74, 76, 85
Amilcar Cabral, 10
Amy Ashwood Garvey, 19
Amy Jacques Garvey, 14, 19
Anglo-Saxon Clubs, 65
anti-colonial, 18
anti-imperial, 18
armed liberation struggle, 14
Asia, 24, 41, 48, 86, 87
Barbadian, 25

Battles of Marne and Verdun, 77
Belgian, 49, 50, 86
Belgium, 59, 82
Black Cross Nurses, 20
Black Ethiopians, 82
black man, 37, 41
Black man's country, 84
black race, 40
black soldiers, 75
bloody war, 82
Booker T. Washington, 37
Brooklyn, 49
brown race, 40, 65
brute force, 14, 46
Cardiff, 75
Central Afrika, 74
Central and South America, 24
Christian, 54, 56, 82
Christians, 54
Civil War, 77
colonialism, 21
Congo, 82
Coptic Church, 56
Cuban, 73
Declaration of rights, 19
Dr. Heinrich Schnee, 72
Dutch, 49
education, 14, 18, 37, 52
Education, 52, 53
Egyptian, 64
English, 49, 85
Ethiopia, 51
Europe, 26, 35, 36, 37, 41, 48, 66, 85, 86, 87
exploitation, 34, 36, 45, 48

extermination, 33, 34
fellowship, 65, 66, 82
Flanders, 50, 53, 85, 86
France, 46, 50, 52, 59, 72, 75, 82, 84, 85, 86
French, 49
Geneva, 75
genocide, 15
German, 49, 72, 75
Germany, 49, 72, 82
Ghandi, 35
government, 17, 25, 35, 46, 47, 48, 51, 67, 73, 75, 78, 81, 83, 89
Henrietta Vinton Davis, 19, 30
history, 14, 15, 27, 53
human rights, 40, 41, 64
humanity, 15, 21, 41, 42, 64, 66, 69, 82, 89
imperialist, 18, 21
independent Afrika, 73
India, 35, 65
International Convention, 46, 75
Irish, 35, 63, 65, 69, 75
Irish independence, 35
Jamaican, 25
Jew, 63, 74, 75, 84
Juvenal A Lopez de C Cabral, 10
Ku Klux Klan, 59
Kwame Nkrumah, 9
Kwame Ture, i
League of nations, 74
League of Nations, 19, 89
Lenin, 67, 68
liberation, 13, 14, 15, 17, 18, 20, 24, 44, 54, 64
Liberia, 74, 83
liberty or death, 15, 50, 86
Lillian Galloway, 19

Liverpool, 85
London, 37, 85
Lora Kofey, 19
Madame De Mena, 19
Madame MLT DeMena, 30
Malcolm X, 10
Manchester, 85
Martin Luther King, 9
Mesopotamia, 50, 77
Mittie Maud Lena Gordon, 19
Mohammedans, 54
monopoly, 36
Mother Afrika, 77, 87
Mr Powell, 65, 69
national government, 21
national independence, 47
Nationalist Party of Ireland, 35
Nationhood, 47
Newport News, 51
Nicene creed, 54
organisation, 13, 14, 15, 18, 19, 20, 30, 45, 46, 47, 49, 50, 51, 52, 53, 55, 56, 58, 64, 65, 69, 71, 75, 78, 83
Pan-Afrikanist, 18, 20, 21
paramilitary, 20
parasite, 82
Patrick Henry, 50, 89
peonage, 41
Pert-em-Hru, v, vi, 6
Poles, 64
powerful Afrika, 73
President General, 71
propaganda, 54, 58, 59, 60, 66, 78
race first, 21
racism, 21
RD Jonas, 58
religious practices, 14

reparations
   Reparations, 15, 72
Revolution, 14, 86
Revolutionary War, 77
Rose Pastor Stokes, 69
Russia, 67, 69
Sankofa360°Ltd, 13
School of Afrikan Philosophy, 19
Senator France, 72
Senator MacCullum, 72
serfdom, 41, 48
sexism, 20
slavery, 48, 55
subjugation, 34
Traitors, 57
Trinidadian, 25
Trotsky, 67
Ukombozii, 13
UNIA, 14, 15, 18, 19, 20, 21, 24, 25, 26, 35, 40, 41, 46, 48, 49, 50, 51, 52, 57, 58, 65, 66, 67, 69, 71, 74, 76, 78, 83, 84, 88
unification, 17
United Nations, 19
unity, 14, 24, 50, 51, 55
Universal Afrikan Motor Corps, 20
Universal Negro Improvement Association & African Communities League, 19
US Satan, 10, 14, 15, 24, 26, 34, 35, 45, 48, 50, 51, 54, 57, 66, 71, 72, 73, 79, 81, 83, 85, 88, 89
Virginia legislature, 89
West Indian, 26, 35, 48, 74, 76, 84, 85
West Indies, 24, 26, 37, 49, 51, 54, 57, 71, 73, 74, 79, 85, 86
white friends, 64, 65
white race, 33, 40, 64, 65, 66
World War I, 14, 84
world's greatest leader, 67
yellow race, 40, 65, 66

Author: Brother Omowale

Spoke some home truths in Britain's Parliament on 17th January 2017. Some sections of the media went berserk as a consequence. Click link for presentation:
https://www.youtube.com/watch?v=Sp-ylYnzbg8

Omowale Ru Pert-em-Hru

Omowale Ru Pert-em-Hru
07933 145 393
Ukombozii@gmail.com

Author of
The Pan-Afrikanism Series

Publications written by Brother Omowale

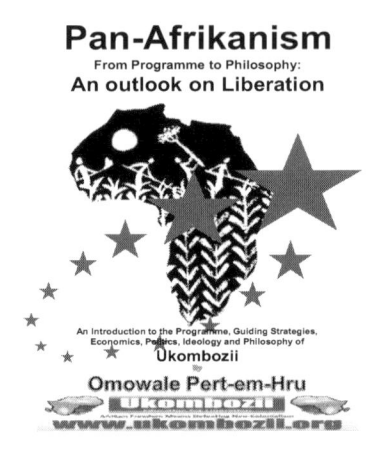

Pan-Afrikanism
From Programme to Philosophy: An outlook on Liberation
By Omowale Pert-em-Hru

Pan-Afrikanism
The Battlefront: Afrikan Freedom Means Defeating Neo-colonialism
By Omowale Pert-em-Hru

Pan-Afrikanism
Material Based Concepts
By Omowale Pert-em-Hru

Drug Economy Attack On Afrikan Youth
We Fight Back!
By Omowale Pert-em-Hru

Pan-Afrikanism: From programme to philosophy

"Pan-Afrikanism: From programme to philosophy" is the only book in the world to provide clear lucid and simple explanations of the liberation strategies of Marcus Garvey, Kwame Nkrumah and Malcolm X. Historians have been naturally concerned with reporting facts of the lives of these great Pan-Afrikanists, but it is for activists to contextualise them in liberation strategies and action plans - a process kick started in it. In addition:

1. It provides a clear succinct explanation of international capitalism's parasitical dependence upon Afrikan people;
2. It provides a clear simple explanation of scientific socialism, relating it to Afrikan principles and culture;
3. It introduces the notion of the greater cycle of revolution which examines and locates revolution not as an incident, but as a process in the context of the entirety of human history;
4. Through an examination of universal principles, it locates the material base of the two opposing sets of ideologies driving human activity and identifies the natural position of Afrikan culture in that milieu; and finally,
5. Through a newly devised set of dialectical tools, it provides a powerfully clear philosophical analysis of matter as a basis for uncovering and understanding the universal laws required for Afrika's liberation.

"Pan-Afrikanism: From programme to philosophy" is a long overdue and much needed source book on the theory of Pan-Afrikanism. For people new to Pan-Afrikanist activism or those who simply want to understand what Pan-Afrikanism is, this book provides clear theoretical guidance. For seasoned cadres and veterans of the Pan-Afrikanist movement, it is a checkpoint/frame of reference for assessing, orientating or even refocusing the trajectory of their activities. Ideally should be studied collectively in groups, particularly those genuinely working towards the liberation of Afrika and her people in the context of worldwide revolution.

Pan-Afrikanism: The Battlefront

When we (Afrikan people) were oppressed under slavery and colonialism our ancestors knew it; they knew that they had to remove these oppressive systems in order to be free. Now we are living in the neo-colonial phase of history and most of us don't know what it is. If we don't know it, we can't understand it; if we can't understand it, we can't consciously do anything to challenge it; if we can't do anything to challenge it, we can't get rid of it; if we can't get rid of it, we're stuck in it; if we're stuck in neo-colonialism, Afrika can't be liberated and we won't be a free and self determining people. The critical task before us therefore, is to raise our collective consciousness of neo-colonialism and how to defeat it in Afrikan communities everywhere. *"Pan-Afrikanism: The Battlefront"* raises our consciousness to better equip us for Afrika's liberation.

"Pan-Afrikanism: The Battlefront" provides a thorough analysis of neo-colonial mechanisms and processes by which the capitalist system arrests Afrikan development in the contemporary world. By facilitating a grounded understanding of how those mechanisms hold us back, it lays the foundation for Afrikan people's corrective actions. It seeks to enhance our understanding by:

1. Introducing readers to some basic concepts of war;
2. Explaining how Afrika's resources was the hidden reason behind World Wars I and II;
3. Linking neo-colonialism to its roots in the enslavement and colonisation of Afrikan people, exposing it as their modern manifestation;
4. Examining the origin, development and intricate workings of neo-colonialism and its adverse impact on Afrikan people;
5. Exposing how a wavering neo-colonialism is altering its form in a desperate and increasingly vicious attempt to increase its life span;
6. Exposing the appointment of President Obama, as an act of counter-insurgency and containment against Afrikan people in quest of liberation; and
7. Exposes Zionism as settler colonialism and genocide, which whilst operating as a junior, but powerful partner in imperialism, actively undermines the interests of Afrikan people.

"Pan-Afrikanism: The Battlefront" should be treated as an introductory and grounding text, laying the foundation for a fuller understanding of the essence of the economic and political problems confronting Afrikan people in the world today. As with the other books in the series, it should be studied collectively in groups, particularly by groups genuinely working towards the liberation of Afrika and her people in the context of worldwide revolution.

Pan-Afrikanism: Material Based Concepts

"Pan-Afrikanism: Material Based Concepts" applies materialist philosophical tools to raise understanding of key Pan-Afrikan concepts such as history, culture, identity and the role of women in Afrika's liberation. Methodologically, Pan-Afrikanists use historical facts rather than imagination as basis for developing theory. *"Pan-Afrikanism: Material Based Concepts"* supplements this working from nature as material base to interpret those historical facts for clearer understanding of Afrikan people's problems and improved strategising. In addition to contextualising and explaining Pan-Afrikanism, it:

1. Clarifies what Pan-Afrikanism is not, referencing dangerously undermining distortions about religion, sexuality and biological make up, wrongly associated with Pan-Afrikanism. This lays the basis for distinguishing it from neo-colonialist and Divisionist imposters misleadingly labelling themselves "Pan-Afrikanists" and clears confusion, allowing Pan-Afrikanism to be properly defined and explained;
2. Explains history contextually, facilitating its proper application for achieving Pan-Afrikanism. History is more than a collection of facts. Historical phases and how they are derived must be understood, if revolution is to be achieved;
3. Explains culture contextually and its proper application for Pan-Afrikanism. At one level, culture is a people's total experience and the failure to understand its source, operation and derivation hinders liberation efforts;
4. Explains identity contextually and its proper interpretation for unity and Pan-Afrikanism. Identity removed from its material base triggers identity confusion as it reduces to 'opinions' and transforms destructively into a source of deep rooted disunity;
5. Takes feminine and masculine principles, locates them in the context of nature as base and uses this to examine and highlight the role of Afrikan women in the liberation process;
6. Succinctly explains the context and basis of racism;
7. Clarifies and explains the symbiotic relationship between Afrikan culture, Pan-Afrikanism and scientific socialism.

"Pan-Afrikanism: Material Based Concepts", is the third in a trilogy of books demystifying and explaining Pan-Afrikanism. For people new to Pan-Afrikanist activism or seeking greater understanding, it adds clarity and theoretical guidance. For seasoned cadres and veterans, it provides a frame of reference for assessing, orientating or even refocusing the trajectory of their activities. As with the others, it should be studied collectively in groups, particularly those genuinely working towards the liberation of Afrika and her people in the context of worldwide revolution.

Drug Economy attack on Afrikan Youth: We Fight Back!

"Drug economy attack on Afrikan youth: We fight back!" uncovers a world where state agencies including bankers and police, manage Britain's dirty money and drug economy hand in hand with Afrikan and other pushers as fronts. This results in the criminalisation of targeted Afrikan youths contained in internal colonies. It:

1. Critically examines state mechanisms and their operations, exposing their inherent violence and the British State's disproportionate violence against Afrikan youths in its home based colonies;
2. Exposes the origins and development of 'Low intensity Warfare'. Widely deployed against Afrikan youth in Britain and other capitalist centres, it was designed by Britain's then leading general Frank Kitson against Afrikan freedom fighters during decolonizing struggles in the 1950's;
3. Unearths underground workings of the multi-billion dollar international drug economy operating in service of capitalism's elite, exposing the corrupt role of banks, police and even governments that impose drug economies on Afrikan youths contained in internal colonies;
4. Reminds of real life cases where Scotland Yard went overseas to recruit known murderers and rapists as mercenaries, paying them handsomely to unofficially police Britain's drug economy attack on contained Afrikan youths. It was no surprise when they raped and murdered whilst 'on duty' in Britain. Police mercenaries' murderous activities are the root source of spiralling gun and knife crime in targeted Afrikan communities;
5. Clarifies Malcolm X's use of the phrase 'by any means necessary'. Criminals posing as freedom fighters abuse the phrase, misleadingly suggesting he supported smuggling drugs to fund 'Afrikan liberation'. This is a lie. His opposition to the drug economy was uncompromising. Some social commentators even suggest he was assassinated by 'the mob' because of it.

Criminality created by the British state's drug economy is used as justification to unleash police terror campaigns in Afrikan internal colonies: Police budgets increase; Gun toting SAS killer soldiers are said to operate on Britain's streets disguised in police uniforms; Unprovoked murders of Afrikan people by police and their agents become increasingly common; Afrikan youths are routinely stopped and searched several times more than any other group; and drug induced state violence is wilfully perpetrated against siege ridden law abiding Afrikan communities. These claims may sound sensational but inside the covers of this book there is compelling evidence to support them.

Publications written by
Brother Omowale

Conceptions and misconceptions of Garvey and Garveyism

In 1914 Marcus Garvey and his fiancée Amy Ashwood co-founded the UNIA – an organisation destined to become the largest international grassroots Afrikan organisation of the 20th century. At its low there were only 13 members following a split in 1917; in 1918 Garvey was calling meetings attracting 3, 5, 7 and over 10 thousand people. By 1919 the UNIA boasted a membership of over 2 million. In 1920 its convention brought 25 thousand into New York's Madison Square Garden's. In 1923 Garvey assessed the membership of the UNIA at 6 million and later reported 11 million.

Its success impressed, not only the minds of Garvey's followers, but their hearts. Years after death he elicits incredible pride and loyalty from Afrikan communities around the world. Unable to erase his legacy, imperialism's intelligence agencies set about distorting it by creating and cascading myths designed to dampen his popularity. *"Conceptions and misconceptions of Garvey and Garveyism"* challenges a number of popularised myths distorting Garvey's legacy:

1. The myth that Garvey was anti-Christian when in fact he was a Christian publicly objecting to the way Europe's elite misused his religion;
2. The myth that Garvey was anti other races and opposed to working in inter-racial solidarity when in fact such alliances were nurtured when deemed appropriate;
3. The myth that it is not possible to simultaneously be a 'Garveyite' and 'Marxist', when in fact the UNIA was a broad grouping which brought together wide ranging political ideologies including the 'Marxists' who brought 'Race First' ideology into the organisation;
4. The myth that Garvey was the prophet of Ethiopia's emperor Haile Selassie despite the fact they developed into bitter ideological enemies, with Garvey brutally and publicly castigating the emperor and the emperor silently plotting his political destruction;
5. The myth that Garvey sought to repatriate all Afrikan people when in fact targeted collective repatriation of some (not all) was an implicit part of the UNIA's liberation strategy; and
6. The myth that Garvey was anti-socialist when in fact he opposed European's racist misrepresentation of socialism.

Whilst historians have reported facts of Garvey's life, it is for activists to deepen understanding of his tremendous contribution by contextualising them into liberation strategies and action plans. *"Conceptions and misconceptions of Garvey and Garveyism"* concludes by outlining the Afrikan liberation strategy of Marcus Garvey and the UNIA.

Strategically selected quotes from Marcus Garvey

"Strategically selected quotes from Marcus Garvey" is intended as a handbook for members of Pan-Afrikan organisations, other activists and students to assist them in the speedy assimilation of Garvey's key strategic ideas. Beyond that it is hoped that it will also contribute by performing a similar role in the wider Afrikan community and among friends and supporters of the wider Afrikan liberation struggle, popularising his ideas in the process.

Centenary of World War, the UNIA and 'Race First'

As its title implies, *"Centenary of World War, the UNIA and 'Race First'"* was written as a commemoration of those 3 important events in Afrikan people's and broader humanity's history. It presents evidence supporting the thesis that Marcus Garvey was the greatest Afrikan grassroots organiser of the twentieth century. It exposes a fake debate which occurred in Britain shortly before the centenary year which misleadingly claimed - in opposition to the historical record - that 'Marxists' cannot be members of the UNIA. It concludes by identifying the origin of 'Race First' as an idea and term, demonstrating that it was brought into the UNIA by what the fake debate wrongly labelled 'Marxist members' of the UNIA.

100 years of Marcus Garvey in the UK

Written to commemorate the 100th anniversary of Marcus Garvey's first arrival in Britain, *"100 years of Marcus Garvey in the UK"* contains Garvey's autobiographical account of his organising activities. It summarises and recounts aspects of his history whilst there. It briefly summarises the essence of Garvey and the UNIA and shows how he successfully married his Christian beliefs with his Pan-Afrikan vision. Finally, it recounts the early history of the Marcus Garvey Organising Committee, set up in Britain in the early 2000's.

Special note:

The following titles have been incorporated into *"Conceptions and misconceptions of Garvey and Garveyism"*: (i) *"Strategically selected quotes from Marcus Garvey"*; (II) *"Centenary of World War, the UNIA and 'Race First'"*; and (iii) *"100 years of Marcus Garvey in the UK"*

Publications written by
Brother Omowale

Afrikan People Abolished The 'Slave Trade'
By Omowale Pert-em-Hru

Horrors, Responsibilities and Origin of Slavery
Omowale Pert-em-Hru
Background for the Parliament Debate

The Beautiful Black Afrikan People Went for a walk

© Omowale Pert-em-Hru, 1998
Reprinted, 2019

Afrikan People Abolished the 'Slave Trade'
British imperialism owes each and every Afrikan person in the world a whopping £615,598,559 Billion first instalment i.e. six hundred and fifteen million, five hundred and ninety eight thousand, five hundred and fifty nine billion pounds - each. The premises/assumptions, formula and calculations are openly stated in *"Afrikan People Abolished the 'Slave Trade'"*.

By combining economic, political and military analysis on the geographical plane, *"Afrikan People Abolished the 'Slave Trade'"* introduces the new **Abolition Matrix tool**, which revolutionises the readers ability to accurately and properly analyse and assess the impact of forces leading to the defeat of slavery. The **Abolition Matrix tool** is supported by a gender balanced, contextually rich rendition of the Haitian revolution. In addition it:

1. Provides a brief insight into the glorious history of Afrikan people before the enslavement era, illustrating how Afrikan genius advanced humanity;
2. Graphically outlines the outrageously inhumane treatment issued to Afrikan people by the wicked enslavers of European imperialism;
3. Examines the thesis that Afrikan people's enslavement was self-inflicted, providing evidence of Afrikan resistance usually excluded from that debate;
4. Exposes evidence indicating William Wilberforce was an anti-abolitionist subversive government agent, tasked with undermining the whole abolition movement and process;
5. Provides lucid, clear and succinct examples of named Afrikan warriors, whose actions forced the abolition of slavery and the misnamed 'Slave Trade';
6. Contextualises slavery as the origin of imperialism's colonisation and neo-colonisation processes; and
7. Identifies the origin and core principles of slavery and anti-slavery social systems, proving that slavery has no implicit connection with Afrikan people and their culture.

"Afrikan People Abolished the 'Slave Trade'" should be treated as an introductory/grounding text, laying the foundation for a fuller understanding of the primary and critical role of Afrikan people in abolishing slavery and the misnamed 'Slave Trade'. As with the other books in the series, it should be studied collectively in groups, particularly by groups genuinely working towards the liberation of Afrika and her people in the context of worldwide revolution.

"The Horrors, Responsibilities and Origin of Slavery" has now been incorporated into *"Afrikan People Abolished the 'Slave Trade'"*.

The Beautiful Black Afrikan People Went for a Walk

Written for children and adults alike, *"The Beautiful Black Afrikan People Went for a Walk"* gives a simple, cogent and clear account of the early history of Afrikan people and humanity, presented as metaphor. Potently written, it clears the fog of centuries of misinformation, turning the perspectives of 'orthodoxy' upside down.

It may come as a deep shock to some but allowing for a little artistic licence, *"The Beautiful Black Afrikan People Went for a Walk"* is a truthful history of humanity made simple. The impact of the ice age on the human family has, for some time, been theorised by anthropologists and related academics. It is widely recognised as instrumental in the diversification of humanity.

Understanding this corrects a plethora of racist distortions, the sum total of which result in Afrikan people being place as a sub-ordinate grouping outside the human family. By identifying Afrikan people as the first inhabitants of all parts of the world and the source from which all other branches are descended, it places them in their correct historical and geographical position as the mothers and fathers of humanity.

By exposing new minds to this truth of history, Afrikan people are presented as a critically important part of the human family and the process of dismantling racism from its root is begun. *"The Beautiful Black Afrikan People Went for a Walk"* is an important learning tool for people of all races, pointing all in the direction of hidden historical truths. A must read for all children of the world, their parents and grandparents, it makes an ideal gift.

For further information about publications contact:

+44 7933 145 393 or

Ukombozii@gmail.com or

Visit the website

www.ukombozii.org

Ukombozii — Education for Liberation
Afrikan Freedom Means Defeating Neo-Colonialism

Omowale
Ru Pert-em-Hru

Omowale Ru Pert-em-Hru is committed to the restoration of justice for Afrikan and other oppressed people of the world. He is founder of Ukombozii, the Pan-Afrikan Society Community Forum (PASCF) and Marcus Garvey & Haitian Revolution Annual Memorial Lectures.

He has been involved in student and community activism since the 1990's, is author of the *Pan-Afrikanism Series* of books and presents the *Pan-Afrikan People's Phone-in* — produced as educational tools for those genuinely interested in the liberation of Afrika. He is Education Coordinator of *Sankofa360ºLtd*.

In acknowledging the primacy of matter he is a philosophical materialist, seeking to contribute to the unification, liberation and development of Afrika and her people under Scientific Socialism — Afrikan people's contribution to worldwide revolution.

www.ukombozii.org

Pan-Afrikan People's Phone-in

Presenter:
Omowale Ru Pert-em-Hru

Mondays 8-10pm

Phone - On air Number:
+44 (0) 203 290 1138

Skype – On air Link:
Panafrikanpeoplesphonein

The Pan-Afrikan People's Phone-in is a space for themed interactive guest based discussion conducted on internet radio. Dealt with from a Revolutionary Pan-Afrikanist perspective, themes focus on issues affecting Afrikan people locally and globally.

Spread the word: Please tell all of your family friends, fellow organisation members, colleagues, associates and other networks about this show.

Printed in Great Britain
by Amazon